I0003404

Understanding HTML, the living standard

or

In my opinion there only is one language for the web

List of Contents

Introduction

This work attempts to explain how to create a web page using HTML, the living standard.

Web pages consist of two parts: the data *(known as the markup)* and the presentation *(known as the style)*. These should be kept quite distinct because should you wish to change (a) something in the data it is difficult to find it if the styles (presentation) are mixed up with the data and (b) by having a separate file for the styles it is easy to change the presentation for the whole page (or even the whole site) very quickly.

So you need two files, one for the data whose file name should finish in *.html* which stands for HyperTest Markup Language and another for the styles whose file name should finish in *.css* which stands for Cascading Style Sheets. I am not going to describe the latter but a good book that I can recommend and use is *Cascading Style Sheets: Designing for the Web* by Håkon Wium Lee and Bert Bos.

Examples:

- if styles are used throughout and within the html markup it is significantly more difficult to change than if this is in a CSS file. The latter involves changing only one line. the former very many lines.
- **all** the text on your web page could be changed from black to red by adding one line only to your CSS file.

However some elements that were previously presentational have been redefined to be media independent (see page 49) [1], for example: `<b>` (see page 67), `<i>` (see page 66), `<hr>` (see page 33), `<s>` (see page 54), `<small>` (see page 53).

It is not my intention to document how the "on" events work although I have listed them (see page 142) nor to discuss building scripts which could be associated to them.

One other comment: Always keep your web pages up-to-date, web pages with broken links or out-of-date information will detract the people you are trying to attract and probably drop you down the ratings for the search engines.

---

1. Media Independent. e.g. Computers, TV sets, tty (especially for deaf people), telephones, aural (speech) & braille based devices. Style sheets, on the other hand can be media dependent, one for screen and another for printing but not much use for speech

HTML, an evolving language

HTML was originally introduced as HTML Tags in 1991 and has since passed through various versions, HTML 2.0 in 1995, HTML3.2 in 1996, HTML 4 in 1997 and HTML 4.01 in 1999. The last two versions varied quite a lot because different browser vendors added different subsets such that a web page that worked well in one browser would not work properly in another, thus you would find comments on web pages like "this page is best viewed with Browser (whatever)".

During 2004 a small group of people who had been attempting to influence the World Wide Web Consortium (W3C) became so dissatisfied with the progress of the development of HTML that they formed a completely independent working group which became known as "WHATWG" (What working group?) or the Web Hypertext Application Technology Working Group. Their aim was to provide a stable, backwards compatible, specification which brought together the various versions of HTML and to add extensions to make it more suitable for application development as well as a serious tightening up of the conformance requirements compared to the earlier versions.

This revision gradually became known as HTML 5 and after two and a half years (in 2006) was accepted by the W3C. However it is intended to keep it up to date without making new versions. So it is now becoming known simply as HTML without any version number.

Changing (updating) your web page to HTML 5 from a previous version won't change the page, everything you had written previously will continue to work, however you can add new elements which weren't in previous versions, you can add structure to your document using `<article>` and `<section>` to make your document more readable to yourself or whoever may be able to update the document.

Another problem the specification had to overcome was what to do when a web page author writes markup (that's the way we describe the programming language) that is incorrect, illogical or 'broken'. In the past it was up to the browser vendor to decide and that led to all sorts of different results depending on the browser you were using. HTML 5 specifies in every conceivable case what should happen so that now you will get the same result in every browser (that supports HTML 5 - and that is happening quite rapidly, even Internet Explorer 9, 10 and 11 will implement HTML 5). Of course this does not encourage authors to write 'well-formed' markup. Which would you prefer to see - A page with the message 'Error' or a page which displays the information? All authors should check the results of their work, although you will see many pages where this has clearly not happened.

I will stop referring to HTML 5, but to HTML, the living standard, or simply HTML since there will not be a version HTML 6. HTML will develop but not as "snapshots", it will grow up as you and I grow up.

What's new in HTML?

- `<Canvas>` is a new element designed to enable 2-dimensional drawing and has many different features. It is simple to use being controlled by Javascript. No longer confined to images, the web designer can use the entire page actively without having to resort to Flash, Silverlight or other add-ons.
- `<Video>` which simplifies the embedding of video clips into your web page with attributes like 'controls' which supply all the controls to play, pause and stop without any more programming.
- `<Audio>`, not surprisingly, is like video but for audio files.
- Improved markup for documents. Pages can now be simply divided up into sections by the use of elements like `<section>`, `<article>`, and `<nav>`. Elements like `<aside>` and `<figure>` also enable a better presentation.
- HTML, the living standard, removes all the presentational stuff like `<font>`, `<bgcolor>` etc and the browser author is recommended to use CSS instead.
- Forms have been greatly improved with the introduction of many new types like `password` which will automatically hide the characters typed on to the screen, `date` and `time` with their special formats, `email` and `url` which will check their validity.
- `<mark>` simplifies highlighting.
- `<meter>` and `<progress>` are useful for showing graphically the progress of events.
- and the first line of your document has been simplified as well to `<!DOCTYPE HTML>`. No more worrying about 'transistional' and 'strict'.
- Browsers are forgiving of errors. Errors in your markup will now be dealt with and treated in the same way by every browser.
- HTML is backwards compatible.
- Many elements don't have to be closed, although for readability and to avoid errors it is advised to do so.
- HTML also supports Drag and Drop.

Start using it, but check what works on your page before releasing it to the general public.

Definition of URL

A URL is a valid web address which either points to another page on the web or points to another place in the same document.

Example, pointing to another document is http://www.traveldevel.org/hotel/ and an example pointing to another place in the same document could be #forms. The latter would be used in this manner: <a href="#forms">Forms</a>. Of course forms would need to identified in its correct location as id="forms" for example: <h2 id="forms">Forms</h2>

Forms

bla, bla, bla

Here follows a description of forms:

clicking the word *forms* in this sentence will take you to the heading *Forms* above.

Here is the markup:

```
<h2 id="forms">Forms</h2>
<p>bla, bla, bla</p>
<p>Here follows a description of <a href="#forms">forms:</a></p>
<p>clicking the word <i>forms</i> in this sentence will take you to
    the heading <i>Forms</i> above.</p>
```

The elements of HTML

1. HTML (see page 8)
2. The Header (see page 9)
3. The Body (see page 16)

Most elements in HTML within the `<body>` of a document are classified either as *block level* elements or *inline* elements. Inline elements are contained *within* block level elements. For example a paragraph (the `<p>` element) is a block level element, whilst the `<em>` element which is used to emphasize some text, and is usually displayed as italics, is an inline element.

Of course there are some exceptions, what would the world be without them!

Attributes

Most elements may have one or several attributes associated with them such as `class`, `id`, `title`, `lang`, `src` and `width`. Some of these are described with the description of each element, however a complete list (see page 125) has been added towards the end of this book.

Structure

Several new structural elements have been introduced into html. `article`, `section`, `main`, `nav`, `address`, `header`, `footer` and `hgroup`.

These elements are intended to bring structure and clarity to your web page but readers will not see any difference in the appearance of the web page they are reading. They will, however, help you to write a better document and so you are encouraged to use them.

You can also add the attribute class (`<element class="xxx">`) where xxx is defined in your CSS file and `element` stands for the element you wish to qualify. This would have been done in the past by writing `<div class="xxx">`, but so many `div`'s can become very confusing.

HTML

The very first line in an 'html' document has been simplified from previous versions of html, no longer do you use 'Transitional' or 'Strict', simply:

<!DOCTYPE HTML>

This should be followed by the `lang` attribute, that is the language code.

The reasons for this are that it can:

- assist search engines
- assist speech synthesizers
- assist spell checkers and grammar checkers
- Help the browser (the User Agent) with the typography

Common language codes are :

- "en" (English)
- "fr" (French)
- "de" (German)
- "it" (Italian)
- "nl" (Dutch)
- "el" (Greek)
- "es" (Spanish)
- "ja" (Japanese)
- "en-US" (the U.S. version of English)
- "en-cockney" (the Cockney version of English)

Example:

<html lang="en">

However it is possible to change the language code in the `<body>` of the document, for example:

<p lang="el">... interpreted as Greek for that paragraph ...</p>

The Header

- head
- title
- base
- link
- meta
- style

Head - the `<head>` element

You need to decide on the Character Encoding for your document. Character Encoding is a method of converting bytes into characters. To validate or display an HTML document, a program must choose a character encoding, usually the following would be most suitable in Western Europe:

<meta charset="utf-8">

Note that with HTML you no longer need to use *http-equiv="content-type" content="text/html;*

Two alternatives for Western Europe are:

<meta charset="ISO-8859-1">

<meta charset="windows-1252">

Title - the `<title>` element

Next you need a title. The title will be displayed in the top status bar each time someone looks at your web page. For example:

     \<title>This is the title of my web page\</title>

There can only be one title element in the header.

Meta - the `<meta>` element

You now need to include a description and keywords of your page. This helps the search engines to rank your page, but don't make these too long or your ranking will drop rather than rise, indeed many search engines no longer use these keywords due to misuse (spam) which has occurred in the past.
Keywords need to be comma separated.

Example:

```
<meta name="description" content="Description of my web page">
```

```
<meta name="keywords" content="running, cross country, fell, road running">
```

Let's add the author as well:

```
<meta name="author" content="Fred Smith">
```

Link - the `<link>` element

We also need to tell the browser where to find the styles and other resources. Let's say that the stylesheet is in the same directory as your markup file and let's call it 'preferred.css':

```
<link rel="Stylesheet" type="text/css" href="preferred.css">
```

The `<link>` element has several possible attributes:

- `rel` can take many values, but the most common are
  - `stylesheet` which imports the stylesheet referenced by the `href` attribute
  - `alternate` which permits the user to choose an alternative stylesheet,

    Example:

    ```
    <link rel="Alternate Stylesheet" type="text/css" href="selective.css">
    ```

    If using Firefox or Opera, for example, this can be done by choosing *View | Page Style*. At present it is not available in Google Chrome, Safari or Internet Explorer.
  - `first` which indicates that the current document is a part of a series
  - `next` which indicates that the current document is a part of a series and that the next document in the series is the referenced document
  - `prev` which indicates that the current document is a part of a series and that the previous document in the series is the referenced document
  - `last` which indicates that the current document is a part of a series and that the last document in the series is the referenced document

For example, consider writing a book, each chapter consisting of its own web page. To pass from one chapter to the next you could use "prev" and "next" as follows:

```
<head>
...
<title>Chapter 3</title>
<link rel="prev" href="chapter2.html">
<link rel="next" href="chapter4.html">
</head>
```

- `type` should have the value "text/css" for stylesheet links.
- `href` which must give the URL of the document to be used.
- `title`. With one exception this is purely advisory, however the exception is important: Should there be two or more alternate style sheet links, the title will enable the user to decide which style sheets are used for which alternative syles. But should the author of the document use two or more style sheets with *<link rel="stylesheet" ... >* then the rule is: No `title` attribute and the link is always used, if there is a `title` attribute then only links with the first `title` attribute given will be used.
- `media`. Most web pages are read by people using a computer screen, but the default value is *media="all"*, however if you wished to have a different presentation for the printer (for example when printing you wished to omit the navigation menu) you could use *media="print"* and supply a suitable CSS file.

  Example:

  <link rel="Alternate Stylesheet" type="text/css" href="print.css" media="print">

  Other possible values include braille, handheld, projection, tty, tv, embossed and speech.
- `hreflang`. The use of this attribute gives the language of the linked resource. It is purely advisory. (see page 8)
- `sizes` gives the sizes of icons for visual media.

In a nut shell:

- if there is no `<title>`, the style sheet will always be used
- if there is a `<title>`, or several stylesheets with the same title, they will be used together, unless:
- there is an, or several, "alternative stylesheets" which, if selected, will be used instead. As stated above, this option only works at present in Firefox and Opera browsers.

The `<base>` element

This element enables authors to specify the address (URL) in which all other internal links, images for example, in the document, are to be found. Only one `<base>` element is permitted in a document.

Example:

>   <base href="http:www.traveldevel.org/hotel/iliessa hotel photos/">

so that when the author wishes to insert a picture, all he/she needs to write is:

>   <img src="viewofhotel/IMG_9204_500.JPG">

instead of:

>   <img src="http:www.traveldevel.org/hotel/iliessa hotel photos/
viewofhotel/IMG_9204_500.JPG">

The `<style>` element

Whilst it is possible and permitted to include styles in the html document, I would highly recommend that all styles be put in a separate CSS file.

There is, however, one instance where styles may be useful and that is when you wish to limit the scope of the style, when `<style scoped>` would be placed within the section in which you wish the style to apply and not within the `<head>` element.

Example:

>   *<article>*
>   *<style scoped>*
>   *.comment p { text-align: right; }*
>   *</style>*
>   *<p class="comment">This text is right aligned</p>*
>   *</article>*

The `title` attribute on `<style>` elements defines `<alternate style sheets>` - See the link element on page 10.

Well, that's the end of the header section, so we must close it by adding:

</head>

Resumé

This is a typical header:

```
<!DOCTYPE HTML>
<html lang="en">
<head>
        <meta charset="utf-8">
        <title>This is the title of my web page</title>
        <base href="http:www.traveldevel.org/hotel/iliessa hotel photos/">
        <meta name="description" content="Description of my web page">
        <meta name="author" content="Fred Smith">
        <link rel="Stylesheet" type="text/css" href="preferred.css">
</head>
```

Only global attributes may be used for the `<head>` element.

Scripts

The `<script>` element

Scripts can be small programs which may be embedded in the html markup. They can also be used to hold data which may be used elsewhere in the document, for example:

```
<script>
function calculate (form) {
  var price = 25;
  if (form.elements, circle)
     price += 10;
  if (form.elements, stalls)
     price += 15;
  form.elements.result.value = price;
}
</script>
```

This could be used in a `<form>` (see page 108)

Scripts which are primarily used in the development of dynamic webpages, may be included within the `<head>` section or within the `<body>` section. They may also be put into a separate file which would be called using the `src` attribute.

The usual scripting language is `javascript` although some of the others include `ecmascript` and `livescript`.

A simple example of JavaScript is:

```
<script>
  document.write("Hello World");
</script>
```

Note that in HTML you don't need to put `type="text/javascript"`, it will assume that it is JavaScript.

A good article on JavaScript can be found in wikipedia.

The `<noscript>` element

Not all browsers support scripting, although most do. Also something can go wrong or scripting may be disabled, so it is possible to have a safeguard. Taking the last example on the previous page, we could add the `<noscript>` element to inform the viewer:

```
<script>
   document.write("Hello World");
</script>
<noscript>Your browser does not support scripting</noscript>
```

However it is generally better to avoid using `<noscript>`, and instead to design the page from being a scriptless page to a scripted page, especially remembering that `<noscript>` is not supported in the XHTML syntax.

The Body

- body
- article
- section
- nav
- aside
- h1, h2, h3, h4, h5 and h6
- hgroup
- header
- footer
- address

A web page can tell a story, it can advertise a product, it can link to other web pages or even move you to different parts of the same page. It can list the results of an event, it can do anything you see on paper and a lot more, but it needs to show the information clearly and needs to be well thought out. It can be divided up into Chapters, into Sections, it can have lists, tables or forms and it can even be interactive.

Let's take these one by one.

The <body> element represents the main content of the document and there is only one <body> element:

<body>

See page 144 for the attributes for the <body> element

Article

For structural clarity a document may be divided into sections, chapters or articles. Don't forget the markup is the data or information you wish to pass to the reader. We are not talking about the presentation which should be handled entirely by the CSS stylesheet.

The `<article>` element

The `<article>` element can be used to divide the document up into separate independant parts. This is recommended for magazine or newspaper articles or other independent items of content. It should be used for a complete or self contained composition, that is a composition which could be extracted entirely and used within another document.

`article's` can be nested, for example, in comments following a blog, each comment being an `article`.

Authors are encouraged to use the `<article>` element instead of the `<section>` element when it would make sense to share the contents of the element.

Consider that in html4 you might have written:

```
<div class="article">
 <div class="section">
  <p>... some text ...</p>
 </div>
 <div class="section">
  <p>... some more text ...</p>
 </div>
</div>
```

In html5 you can write:

```
<article>
 <section>
  <p>... some text ...</p>
 </section>
 <section>
  <p>... some more text ...</p>
 </section>
</article>
```

In html4 I used to add, after the `</div>` a comment, such as 'end of Section' or 'end of Article'.

- Attributes for the `<article>` element:
  - ∘ global attributes

Sections

The `<section>` element

Like Articles, the document can be split up into sections:

<section>

... some content then ...

</section>

The `section` element is appropriate if the elements could be listed in a contents list of the document.

Typically each section would have a heading.

There can be several sections. Examples of sections would be chapters, the various tabbed pages in a tabbed dialog box or the numbered sections of a thesis. A web site's home page could be split into sections for an introduction, news items and contact information.

What is the effective difference between `<section>` and `<article>`? Probably none, but it certainly helps from the point of view of clarity in the html document. I would recommend only using the `<section>` element within an `<article>`, thus breaking the article up into sections. Not the other way round.

When an element is needed only for styling purposes, authors should use the `<div>` element.

Example:

<article>
 <section>
  <h1>Chapter 1</h1>
  <p>Fred came to visit Ellen</p>
 </section>
 <section>
  <h1>Chapter 2</h1>
  <p>Fred and Ellen went to watch a rugby match</p>
 </section>
</article>

- Attributes for the `<section>` element:
    - global attributes
    - the `cite` attribute (see page 148)

Navigation

The `<nav>` element

If your web site consists of several pages then you are advised to have a menu, a navigational menu.

Like sections, this can be considered as another section, but it is a special section and for this we use the special element `<nav>`.
For example:

```
<h2>Navigation</h2>
<nav>
 <ul>
  <li><a href="#html">HTML</a></li>
  <li><a href="#header">The Header</a></li>
  <li><a href="#body">The Body</a></li>
 </ul>
</nav>
```

Using CSS, this menu could be placed anywhere on the page, it could even remain fixed whilst the reader scrolls the page. Typically it would normally be placed on the left hand side or near the top of the page. For examples see http://www.whatwg.org/specs/ (top) or http://www.managers-net.com/home.html (left).

Only global attributes may be used for the `<nav>` element.

It cannot be used inside the element `main` (see page 47).

Aside

The `<aside>` element

Consider a conversation between a group of people. During this discussion one person makes a remark to another member of the group, often referred to as 'an aside'. Putting this on paper (or a web page) this might be represented as a 'bubble' or a little box separated from the text. To do this you could put some code into the CSS file describing how to display the element `<aside>`. For example, consider this text:

Did you know that William Shakespeare wrote plays about Henry IV, Henry V, Henry VI and Henry VIII, but not Henry VII. However Sir Francis Bacon wrote about Henry VII.
(aside) Did Bacon write all the plays ascribed to Shakespeare?

On a web page this could be written:

```
<p><em>Did you know that William Shakespeare wrote plays about
Henry IV, Henry V, Henry VI and Henry VIII, but not Henry VII.
However Sir Francis Bacon wrote about Henry VII.</em></p>
<aside>Did Bacon write all the plays ascribed to Shakespeare?</aside>
```

and with a bit of help from CSS this could appear as:

Did you know that William Shakespeare wrote plays about Henry IV, Henry V, Henry VI and Henry VIII, but not Henry VII. However Sir Francis Bacon wrote about Henry VII.

> Did Bacon write all the plays ascribed to Shakespeare?

Only global attributes may be used for the `<aside>` element.

It cannot be used inside the element `main` (see page 47).

Address

The `<address>` element

The `<address>` element might be a little misleading. It should only by used to show contact information for the section to which it refers or if it applies to the `<body>` element (that is the whole web page, not the web **site**), then it applies to the whole document (the web page). It should not be used for ordinary postal addresses, unless they are the contact addresses for that section. (The `<p>` element is the appropriate element for marking up such addresses).

Example, using fictitious links showing contact information about a page concerning 'The Pareto effect':

```
<address>
 <a href="../contacts/key_people/John Jones</a>,
 <a href="../contacts/key_people/Pierre Smith</a>,
  contact persons concerning <a href="paretoanalysis">Pareto Analysis</a>
</address>
```

Typically it would be included with other information in a `<footer>` element.

Only global attributes may be used for the `<address>` element.

Header

The `<header>` element

The `<header>` element typically contains a form of introduction, a title or a group of titles. It could be the header of a table of contents or even a search form. Example:

```
<header>
 <h1>Understanding HTML, the living standard</h1>
</header>
```

```
<header>
 <h1>Colourless green ideas sleep furiously</h1>
 <p>An example of a syntactically correct sentence, even if it makes no sense.</p>
</header>
```

A `<header>` element typically contains an `<h1>` — `<h6>` or an `<hgroup>` element.

Only global attributes may be used for the `<header>` element.

The `<h1>`, `<h2>`, `<h3>`, `<h4>`, `<h5>` and `<h6>` elements

These elements represent headings for their sections.

The first heading should use the `<h1>` element, a sub heading should use the `<h2>` element. Just because you would like to see the second heading have a larger font then the first heading is not a reason to start with the `<h2>` element and use the `<h1>` element below it. If you really want that effect then use the CSS to style these elements to render that. Remember the `<h1>` element is said to have the highest rank, `<h2>` a smaller rank down to the `<h6>` element which has the lowest rank.

Example:

```
<body>
  <h1>Managers-Net Archives</h1>
    <h2>Pareto Analysis</h2>
      <article>
        <h3>The Pareto effect</h3>
          <p>A history of Vilfredo Pareto ...</p>
        <h3>The Pareto chart</h3>
          <img src="chart.jpg">
        <h3>Some problems</h3>
          <ul>
            <li>... a list of problems ...</li>
          </ul>
        <h3>In conclusion</h3>
          <p>Some text</p>
      </article>
</body>
```

Personally I always use <h1> for the heading of my web page and never use it on that page again. I format it using CSS and use the same heading for every page on that web site.

Only global attributes may be used for these elements.

The `<hgroup>` element

The `<hgroup>` element is a structural element and will not have any effect on the web page your readers will see.

This element is intended to group headings together so that if you were to produce an outline of your document, only the most important heading would be shown.

Only the elements `<h1>` to `<h6>` can be used within an `<hgroup>`

Example:

```
<body>
<hgroup>
<h1>HTML, The living standard</h1>
<h2>In my opinion there is only one language for the web</h2>
</hgroup>
...
</body>
```

It would be just as correct to write this as:

```
<body>
<header>
<h1>HTML, The living standard</h1>
<p>In my opinion there is only one language for the web</p>
</header>
...
</body>
```

You could even have included a third header `<h3>` (or more, to `<h6>`) within the `<hgroup>` if you had so wished.

It would be pointless to include either the `<hgroup>` or the `<header>` elements if you only had one header (e.g. `<h1>`) within the header

For example:

```
<body>
<h1>HTML, The living standard</h1>
...
</body>
```

The example on the previous page could be modified to include the `<hgroup>` element:

```
<body>
  <hgroup>
   <h1>Managers-Net Archives</h1>
   <h2>Pareto Analysis</h2>
  </hgroup>
  <article>
   <h3>The Pareto effect</h3>
     <p>A history of Vilfredo Pareto ...</p>
   <h3>The Pareto chart</h3>
     <img src="chart.jpg">
   <h3>Some problems</h3>
     <ul>
       <li>... a list of problems ...</li>
     </ul>
   <h3>In conclusion</h3>
     <p>Some text</p>
  </article>
</body>
```

Only global attributes may be used for the `<hgroup>` element.

Footer

The `<footer>` element

The `<footer>` element typically contains items like References, Links to further reading, Links to related topics and the Author for the Section to which it applies. It is not intended for items such as appendices nor indexes. Contact information for this section should be marked up using the `<address>` element.

Example:

```
<section>
<h2>What's in a Name?</h2>
<p>Concerning the Shaker of the Spear,
        Of Pallas Athene, the classical goddess,
        Of Wisdom, War, and Invention</p>
<footer>
<p>References:</p>
<ul>
 <li><cite>A Short History of Education</cite> by J.W.Adamson</li>
</ul>
<p>Related topics</p>
<ul>
 <li>Works by William Shakespeare</li>
 <li>Works by Francis Bacon</p>
</ul>
<p>Further reading:</p>
<ul>
 <li><cite>The Prince of Poets</cite> by S.A.E.Hickson</li>
</ul>
<p>Author:</p>
<ul>
 <li>Fred Smith</li>
</ul>
</footer>
</section>
```

Another example of a footer is:

```
<footer>
<p>Published <time datetime="2014-01-14T14:07:00">on
        2014/01/14 at 2:07pm</time></p>
<p>Copyright &copy; 2014 Fred Smith</p>
</footer>
```

Which would look like this:

Published on 2014/01/14 at 2:07pm
Copyright © 2014 Fred Smith

Only global attributes may be used for the `<footer>` element.

Resumé

The `article` element is like a wrapper for the whole document whilst the `main` element can be used as a container for the dominant contents of the document.

`section` can divide the document into chapters[2] , for example.

`nav` is another part of a document used for the list of its contents.

The `aside` represents a section of a page that consists of content that is tangentially related to the subject.

`h1` - `h6` are used for the various headings of the document.

`hgroup` - the heading of a section. It can only contain the elements `h1` - `h6`.

The `header` element is typically a form of introduction or title whilst the `footer` element typically contains information about the author of the document, links to related documents and copyright data etc.

A comment on an article is not part of the `article` on which it is commentating. It is its own article.

---

2. chapters, various tabbed pages, numbered sections of a thesis or the various sections of a web page.

Grouping content

- p
- hr
- pre
- blockquote
- ol
- ul
- li
- dl
- dt
- dd
- figure
- figcaption
- main
- div

Paragraphs

The <p> element

The <p> element represents a paragraph which may contain inline markup (see page 49) but not other grouping content.

Example[3]:

```
<p>the threshing out of particulars and, after eliminating errors, arranging
them in logical order, each part supporting the other
as incontestable fact beneficially instead of each man
blindly worshipping his own idols and preconceptions.
It is this very principle of induction that gives Parliament,
with its committees and reports, its intrinsic
power, and <em>Bacon-Shakespeare</em> was a member of it
for twenty five years.</p>
```

The following is an example using lists. Note that lists cannot be part of the <p> element so they follow the paragraph but are not part of it.

These are the starting times for the "White Horse Relay" which used to be held in Wiltshire. It covered 75 miles:

- 09:00 at Knoll Down (near Cherhill White Horse)
- 10:00 from Broad Hinton
- 10:44 from Marlborough

3. The Prince of Poets, page 7

- *11:08 from Knap Hill (near Alton Barnes White Horse)*
- *11:53 from Pewsey*
- *12:36 from Upavon*
- *13:34 from Gore Cross*
- *14:30 from Bratton Recreation Ground*
- *15:15 from Seend Head*
- *16:04 from Devizes White Horse*

The first runner could be expected to finish at about 16:35 and the last around 17:15

Below is the markup:

<p>These are the starting times for the "White Horse Relay" which used to be held in Wiltshire. It covered 75 miles:</p>
<ul>
*   <li>09:00 at Knoll Down (near Cherhill White Horse)</li>*
*   <li>10:00 from Broad Hinton</li>*
*   <li>10:44 from Marlborough</li>*
*   <li>11:08 from Knap Hill (near Alton Barnes White Horse)</li>*
*   <li>11:53 from Pewsey</li>*
*   <li>12:36 from Upavon</li>*
*   <li>13:34 from Gore Cross</li>*
*   <li>14:30 from Bratton Recreation Ground</li>*
*   <li>15:15 from Seend Head</li>*
*   <li>16:04 from Devizes White Horse</li>*
</ul>
<p>The first runner could be expected to finish at about 16:35 and the last around 17:15</p>

An alternative way to markup this example would be to use the `<div>` element instead of two `<p>` elements as follows:

<div>These are the starting times for the "White Horse Relay" which used to be held in Wiltshire. It covered 75 miles:
<ul>
*   <li>09:00 at Knoll Down (near Cherhill White Horse)</li>*
*   <li>10:00 from Broad Hinton</li>*
*   <li>10:44 from Marlborough</li>*
*   <li>11:08 from Knap Hill (near Alton Barnes White Horse)</li>*
*   <li>11:53 from Pewsey</li>*
*   <li>12:36 from Upavon</li>*
*   <li>13:34 from Gore Cross</li>*
*   <li>14:30 from Bratton Recreation Ground</li>*
*   <li>15:15 from Seend Head</li>*
*   <li>16:04 from Devizes White Horse</li>*
</ul>

The first runner could be expected to finish at about 16:35 and the last around 17:15</div>

Only global attributes may be used for the <p> element.

The `<hr>` element

The `<hr>` element represents a break between paragraphs, a thematic break or a transistion to another topic

Unless it has a styling change (usually made in a CSS document) it is represented by a straight horizontal line across the page.

This element does not have an end tag, that is it finishes with the > character. It may have one or more global attributes before the >

Example:

Chapter 3

Bertie continued through the forest where ...

The markup would be:

```
<h2>Chapter 3</h2>
<hr>
<p>Bertie continued through the forest where ... </p>
```

Only global attributes may be used for the `<hr>` element.

The `<pre>` element

The `<pre>` element represents a block of preformatted text, it is often used to show fragments of computer code. It could also be used to display ASCII art, for example:

```
<pre>
              _____
         /   |   \
        /    |    |
   _____    .....      ||
      /                 |    (I'm not a very good artist!)
     |___o_____o__|      triangular wheels!
         0 0        0 0
</pre>
```

<p>The following example is a small program to calculate and display all prime numbers between 1 and 30,000. The algorithm of the program is to start out with an array containing representatives for all odd numbers between 3 and 29,999. Starting from 3 and working upwards, each odd number is then tested. If a number is still a member of the list when it is tested, it is a prime number, and thus it is printed, and all odd multiples of the number are eliminated from the list. As can be expected, the program is quite slow on calculating the very first primes, but from then on it gets faster and faster. Note that 1 and 2 are assumed to be primes, and not actually calculated.<p>

```
<pre>
Program Primes; (*R-*)
const
  max2 = 15000; (* maxprime/2 *)
  max3 = 10000; (* maxprime/3 *)

var
  i, j, k: integer;
  test: array[2..max2] of boolean;

begin
  write(1:8,2:8);
  for i:=2 to max2 do test[i]:=true;
  for i:=2 to max2 do
  if test[i] then
  begin
   j:=i+i-1; write(j:8);
   if j<max3 then
   begin
    k:=i+j;
     while k<=max2 do
```

```
    begin
      test[k]:=false; k:=k+j;
    end;
   end;
  end;
   writeln;
  end.
</pre>
```

Notice that using `<pre>` also preserves the formatting.

Only global attributes may be used for the `<pre>` element.

The `<blockquote>` element

The `<blockquote>` element represents a paragraph or paragraphs taken from another source and the source, if known as a valid URL, should be cited using the `cite` attribute.

Example:

```
<p>Samuel Hickson wrote about Shakespeare (or Bacon)
   in <cite>The Prince of Poets</cite>:</p>
<blockquote cite="http://www.sirbacon.org/hickson.htm">
   Thus did the stricken muse of England's newly
   budding and lovely rose sing his farewell to his Princess
   of France, his lovely Marguerite, his Daiselorn. He
   pulled out whatever stumps of despised love still stuck
   painfully in his gums, and turned once more soberly
   to the achievements of the dreams of his youth, ...
</blockquote>
```

Quotes should not be used within `<blockquote>`, since it is implicitly already a quotation.

The resulting text would look like this:

Samuel Hickson wrote about Shakespeare (or Bacon) in *The Prince of Poets*:

> Thus did the stricken muse of England's newly budding and lovely rose sing his farewell to his Princess of France, his lovely Marguerite, his Daiselorn. He pulled out whatever stumps of despised love still stuck painfully in his gums, and turned once more soberly to the achievements of the dreams of his youth, ...

Lists

There are various ways of displaying lists. They can be ordered <ol>, unordered <ul> or description lists <dl>

The <ol> element, used for numbered lists

To have any sense it must contain <li> items (see below) and these items will be numbered (by default) in numerical ascending order in the order in which they have been written starting with 1 (one). It is possible to reverse this order by adding the reversed attribute and also to start from a different point using the start attribute. If the reversed attribute is used (<ol reversed>) the list will remain in the same order as it was written, but if there are 14 items in the list, it will start with the number 14.

It is also possible to use letters or roman numerals instead of numbers by using the type attribute.

Keys for the type attribute:

Keyword	Description	Example
1	Decimal numbers	1. 2. 3. 4. etc
a	Lowercase latin alphabet	a. b. c. d. etc
A	Uppercase latin alphabet	A. B. C. D. etc
i	Lowercase roman numerals	i. ii. iii. iv. etc
I	Uppercase roman numerals	I. II. III. IV. etc

Example, using the start attribute:

```
<h2>B</h2>
<ol>
 <li>Bedfordshire</li>
 <li>Berkshire</li>
 <li>Buckinghamshire</li>
</ol>
<h2>C</h2>
<ol start=4>
 <li>Cambridgeshire</li>
 <li>Cheshire</li>
 <li>Cleveland</li>
 <li>Cornwall</li>
 <li>Cumbria</li>
</ol>
```

This would normally display thus:

B

1. Bedfordshire
2. Berkshire
3. Buckinghamshire

C

4. Cambridgeshire
5. Cheshire
6. Cleveland
7. Cornwall
8. Cumbria

The `<ul>` element, used for unordered or bulleted lists

This is used for lists where order has no importance, for example:

```
<h2>Some early HICKSONs</h2>
<ul>
<li>William de Hustedon, born ca 1040 in England, died 1105
 - forerunner of the Hickson/Hixons.</li>
<li>Thomas Hickson, born before 1380.
  Thomas was named in <q>A Middlewich Chartulary</q> as
  a Chamberlain for 1403-4 and again for 1407-8 for Middlewich.
  A burgess of Middlewich in 1414/15.
</li>
<li>Hugh Hickson, born ca. 1380.
  A butcher of Middlewich.
</li>
<li>Stephen Hickson, born before 1381.
  He was Lord of the Manor and is recorded as having lands in Cheshire
  in 1381.
</li>
</ul>
```

In your browser this list should look like this: (Note, All examples are shown in grey, bold and italic, *thus*)

Some early HICKSONs

- *William de Hustedon, born ca 1040 in England, died 1105 - forerunner of the Hickson/Hixons.*
- *Thomas Hickson, born before 1380. Thomas was named in "A Middlewich Chartulary" as a Chamberlain for 1403-4 and again for 1407-8 for Middlewich. A burgess of Middlewich in 1414/15.*
- *Hugh Hickson, born ca. 1380. A butcher of Middlewich.*
- *Stephen Hickson, born before 1381. He was Lord of the Manor and is recorded as having lands in Cheshire in 1381.*

The bullets (dots) shown before each item can be changed to other shapes by using CSS.

Unlike the `<ol>` element, the `<ul>` element should be used where the order of the items is not important.

Only global attributes may be used for the `<ul>` element.

The `<li>` element, (list item)

This element is to be used for each item in a list whether it be an ordered or unordered list. Examples have been shown above.

It should be noted that the `type` attribute is not allowed on the `<li>` element and the `value` attribute could be used with the `<li>` element in an ordered list instead of using the `start` attribute of the `<ol>` element.

Lists within lists, or nested lists.

If you wanted to list all the photographs which you took on your tour of the world, you start by listing all the places, and then insert a list of the photographs under each place, for example:

- Australia
  - Kangaroos
  - Penguins
  - Emus
- New Zealand
  - Yellow Gorse
  - Lupins
  - Sheep
  - Inter Island Ferry

Then you could use this markup:

```
<ul>
<li>Australia
 <ul>
  <li>Kangaroos</li>
  <li>Penguins</li>
  <li>Emus</li>
 </ul>
</li>
<li>New Zealand
 <ul>
  <li>Yellow Gorse</li>
  <li>Lupins</li>
  <li>Sheep</li>
  <li>Inter Island Ferry</li>
 </ul>
</li>
</ul>
```

Note that the closing `</li>` comes **after** the completion of the interior list and not before it.

Here is an example of the value attribute taken from the list of results for a race in which only the members of my club have been listed, with their times and finishing positions within the event: *(the names have been changed)*

```
<figure>
  <figcaption>Sunday 10th August: Roundway Rampage</figcaption>
  <ol>
    <li value="14">53:49 James Dodwell</li>
    <li value="19">58:09 Matthew Pemberton</li>
    <li value="29">64:06 Robert Osman</li>
    <li value="31">65:08 Ann Hickson</li>
    <li value="35">66:37 Able Johnson</li>
    <li value="57">87:33 Fred Smith</li>
  </ol>
</figure>
```

and the resulting webpage:

Sunday 10th August: Roundway Rampage
14. 53:49 James Dodwell
19. 58:09 Matthew Pemberton
29. 64:06 Robert Osman
31. 65:08 Ann Hickson
35. 66:37 Able Johnson
57. 87:33 Fred Smith

Note the way that the list has been given a title by using the <figure> and <figcaption> elements.

The `<dl>` element, (description list)

This is used with `<dt>` and `<dd>` elements in the same way as `<ol>` and `<ul>` elements surround `<li>` elements and like them must always be closed (in this case with `</dl>`).

It is inappropriate for dialogues or conversations, but it could be used where something (the `<dt>` item) needs a description or where a term needs explaining.

Only global attributes may be used for the `<dl>` element.

The `<dt>` element

... which I like to think of as the term or name of the item which is being described.

Only global attributes may be used for the `<dt>` element.

The `<dd>` element

... represents the description, defintion or value of the above item.

For example, a description list could be used to list the authors of books who have discussed the Shakespeare/Bacon controversy:

Brig.-Gen. Samuel Arthur Einem Hickson
The Prince of Poets or What's in a name?

Mrs Henry Pott
Francis Bacon and his Secret Society

W.F.C.Wigston
A New Study of Shakespeare

Francis Bacon: Poet, Prophet, Philosopher

E G Harman
Francis Bacon and his Impersonations

Sir E Durning Lawrence
Bacon is Shakespeare

which would be marked up as:

<dl>
<dt>Brig.-Gen. Samuel Arthur Einem Hickson</dt>

```
    <dd>The Prince of Poets or What's in a name?</dd>
  <dt>Mrs Henry Pott</dt>
    <dd>Francis Bacon and his Secret Society</dd>
  <dt>W.F.C.Wigston</dt>
    <dd>A New Study of Shakespeare</dd>
    <dd>Francis Bacon: Poet, Prophet, Philosopher</dd>
  <dt>E G Harman</dt>
    <dd>Francis Bacon and his Impersonations</dd>
  <dt>Sir E Durning Lawrence</dt>
    <dd>Bacon is Shakespeare</dd>
</dt>
```

Notice that Wigston wrote two books and so has two `<dd>` entries.

Only global attributes may be used for the `<dd>` element.

Dialogues or Conversations

When marking up a conversation, a dialogue or a scene from a play, you are not describing the speaker, you are quoting the conversation or words.

HTML does not have any elements to do this specifically. One of the recommended ways is to use the element `<p>` and punctuation, but other listing elements, as described on previous pages may be just as suitable. Use of inline elements, described later, such as the `<b>` and `<i>` elements are often suitable.

Here is an example of dialogue taken from Shakespeare [4]:

King Henry

My Lord of Somerset, what youth is that

Of whom you seem to have so tender care?

Somerset

My liege, it is young Henry, Earl of Richmond.

King Henry

Come hither, England's hope. If secret powers

Suggest but truth to my divining thoughts,

This pretty lad will prove our country's bliss;

His looks are full of peaceful majesty.

4. Henry VI, Part III, Act IV, sc vi

The `<figure>` element

A `<figure>` element is a container that allows you to include an image, code listing, poem etc and, optionally, its caption, which can be moved away from the main flow of the document without affecting the document's meaning.

and

The `<figcaption>` element

which represents a caption or legend for the rest of the contents of the `<figure>` element.

Example 1:

A flying fish

would be markup up like this:

```
<figure>
  <img src="/jpeg/sea2.jpg" alt="dolphin jumping out of the water">
  <figcaption>A flying fish</figcaption>
</figure>
```

See also the example of the `<figure>` element used as a container for text on page 41.

Example 2:

Research has been carried out to establish whether the family was entitled to a coat of __Arms__. The result proved surprising but the Arms were incorrectly drawn and should have had a wreath between the crest and the Arms

Family Crest. The motto Fide et Fortitudine is not shown at the College of Arms

The original crest did not include the trefoil which was added for the Irish branch of the family.

The markup:

```
<p>Research has been carried out to establish whether the family was entitled
    to a coat of <a href="#arms">Arms</a>.
    The result proved surprising but the Arms were incorrectly drawn and
    should have had a wreath between the crest and the Arms</p>
<figure id="arms">
<figcaption>Family Crest. The motto <cite>Fide et Fortitudine</cite>
is not shown at the College of Arms</figcaption>
<img src="/crest2.gif"
    alt="Crest of the Irish branch of the Hickson family">
</figure>
<p>The original crest did not include the trefoil which was added for
    the Irish branch of the family.</p>
```

... and an example of a poem:

Shakespeare/Bacon never wearied of quoting Ovid. One famous passage of the **_Metamorphoses_** *of A Golding's translation appears in **_The Tempest_** almost verbatim*[5]

> *Ye elves of hills, brooks, standing lakes and groves,*
> *And ye that on the sands with printless foot*
> *Do chase the ebbing Neptune, ...*
>
> *Ye Ayres and windes; ye Elves of hills, of Brooks, of woods;*
> *Of standing Lakes, and of the Night, approach ye every one.*

and the markup:

```
<p>Shakespeare/Bacon never wearied of quoting Ovid.
    One famous passage of the
    <a href="#ovid"><cite>Metamorphoses</cite></a>
    of A Golding's translation appears in <a href="#shakespeare">
    <cite>The Tempest</cite></a>almost verbatim</p>
<figure id="shakespeare"><blockquote>Ye elves of hills, brooks,
                standing lakes and groves,<br>
                And ye that on the sands with printless foot<br>
                Do chase the ebbing Neptune, ...</blockquote>
</figure>
<figure id="ovid">
    <blockquote>
            Ye Ayres and windes; ye Elves of hills,
            of Brooks, of woods;<br>
            Of standing Lakes, and of the Night, approach ye every one.
    </blockquote>
</figure>
```

Only global attributes may be used for the `<figure>` element.

5. *The Tempest, Act V, sc i*

The `<main>` element

The `<main>` element which is another structural element, can be used as a container for the dominant contents of the document, or of the web page.

A typical document [6] could consist of the following:

```
<article>
  <h3>Job Evaluation - What is it ?</h3>
  <p>Job evaluation is a practical technique, designed to enable
     trained and experienced staff to judge the size of one job relative
     to others. It does not directly determine pay levels, but will
     establish the basis for an internal ranking of jobs.</p>
  <p>The two most common methods of job evaluation that have been
     used ...
     ... three major factors - know how, problem solving and accountability.</p>
  <main>
  <h3>Some Principles of Job Evaluation</h3>
  <ul>
    <li>Clearly defined and identifiable jobs must exist.
       These jobs will be accurately described in an agreed job description.</li>
    <li>All jobs in an organisation will be evaluated using
       an agreed job evaluation scheme.</li>
    <li>Job evaluators ...</li>
  </ul>
  </main>
  <h3>Job Evaluation - The Future</h3>
  <p>As organisations constantly evolve and new organisations emerge
     there will be challenges to existing principles of job evaluation.
     Whether existing job evaluation techniques ...</p>
  <p>Job evaluation is essentially one part of a tripartite subject, which
     is collectively referred to as Job Study ...
     ... is committing the company for ten years.</p>
</article>
```

Generally, the `main` element is redundant with just marking up the page correctly with the other elements. It's mostly only useful as a replacement for `<div` class="content"> or `<div` class="main"> or whatever you use if you want to style the inside of an element separate from its header and footer.

6. taken from http://www.managers-net.com/job_evaluation.html

The `<div>` element

Sometimes there comes a need for a section of the web page to have some special style or properties attached to it and there is no appropriate block level elements such as `<p>` to use. This is when the `<div>` element can come in useful.

`<div>` has no special meaning but it can be used with the `class`, `lang` and `title` attributes. However it should never be used without other elements in the markup and should be used as a last resort. Note that for inline markup the `<span>` element should be used in these situations.

Only global attributes may be used for the `<div>` element.

Text level semantics or inline elements

- a
- em
- strong
- small
- s
- cite
- q
- dfn
- abbr
- ruby
- rt
- rp
- data
- time
- code
- var
- sub
- sup
- span
- i
- b
- u
- mark
- br
- wbr
- samp
- kbd
- bdi
- bdo

The `<a>` element

Also known as an anchor tag, it represents a hyperlink when used with the `href` attribute, used to link to another page within the present document or to another web page on another web site. Without the `href` attribute it can also be used as a placeholder for where a link might otherwise have been placed, if it had been relevant. The `<a>` element may also be wrapped around entire paragraphs, lists, tables, and so forth, even entire sections, provided that there is no interactive content included. When used with the hash sign (#) it can be used to move the reader to another location within the present document.

Examples:

```
<p>Game theory is concerned with
  <a href="http.www.managers-net.org/decisionmaking.html">
  decision making</a> and strategy
  and is used where there is conflict against an opponent such as
  <a href="#rival">rival organizations</a>.</p>
<nav>
<ul>
 <li><a href="/">Home Page</a></li>
 <li><a>Latest news</a></li>
 <li><a href="http://ad.example.com">
   <section>
    <p>This is the best ad you have ever seen</p>
    <p>You are welcome to copy it</p>
   </section>
  </a>
 </li>
</ul>
</nav>
<p id="rival">Rival organizations don't make good decisions.</p>
```

- Attributes for the `<a>` element:
    - global attributes
    - `href`

  and if the `href` attribute is present, then also:
    - `target`
    - `download`
    - `ping`
    - `rel`
    - `hreflang`
    - `type`

The `<em>` element

The `<em>` element represents stress emphasis of its contents and the placing of the emphasis can change the meaning of the sentence.

For example:

> *`<p><em>John</em> said that it was raining.</p>`*

John said that it was raining.

Did *John* really say it or was it someone else?

> *`<p>John <em>said</em> that it was raining.</p>`*

John *said* that it was raining.

Did he really say it?

> *`<p>John said that it <em>was</em> raining.</p>`*

John said that it *was* raining.

But it still *is* raining.

> *`<p>John said that it was <em>raining</em>.</p>`*

John said that it was *raining*.

Raining? - But the ground is not wet.

The level of importance can be increased by extra `<em>` elements:

> *`<p>This, <em>I want to point out, <em>is really important</em></em></p>`*

This, *I want to point out, **is really important***

However the `<em>` element isn't intended to convey importance, and the above line would be better written using the `<strong>` element:

> *`<p>This, <em>I want to point out, <strong>is really important</strong></em></p>`*

This, *I want to point out, **is really important***

Only global attributes may be used for the `<em>` element.

The `<strong>` element

The `<strong>` element represents strong importance, seriousness, or urgency for its contents.

Unlike the `<em>` element it does not change the meaning of a sentence, it is intended to bring certain parts of the text to the reader's attention more quickly, for example:

Warning. Beware or unexploded bombs

The markup is:

```
<p><strong>Warning.</strong> Beware or unexploded bombs</p>
```

Like `<em>`, the level of importance can be increased by repeated use of the `<strong>` element.

<small>Warning</small> Warning **Warning**

The markup for this is:

```
<p><strong>Warning <strong>Warning <strong>Warning</strong>
  </strong></strong></p>
```

and the following code had been added to the CSS file:

strong strong { font-size: 130%; }

CSS note: if the CSS code:

strong { font-size: 130%; }

had been used, every time the `<strong>` element occurred, the markup would have been increased by 130% even if only one occurrence of the `<strong>` element occurred.

Only global attributes may be used for the `<strong>` element.

The `<small>` element

Typical use would be the **small print** often found in documents containing disclaimers, legal restrictions, caveats, copyrights and sometimes to work attributed to an artist or other source.

It does not reduce the emphasis or importance of text marked with the `<em>` or `<strong>` elements.

Example:

`<p>The price of the saucepan is £17 <small>excluding V.A.T.</small></p>`

The `<small>` element is not the same as the `<aside>` element which can also have a `<small>` element included in it.

Only global attributes may be used for the `<small>` element.

The `<s>` element

Do not confuse this element with the `<del>` element (see page 77).

The `<s>` element should be used to show that the text is no longer accurate or relevant.

The `<del>` element should be used when editing a document to indicate text that has been removed.

Examples:

1. using the `<s>` element:

> Buy from us
> ~~was £250.00~~
> now £129.00

2. using the `<del>` element to correct a script:

> ... he travelled to Germany with his cousin, ~~Charles Darwin~~ <u>Philip Sydney</u>, who joined the embassy ...

The markup is:

1. using the `<s>` element:

> *Buy from us*
> *<s>was £250.00</s>*
> *now £129.00*

2. using the `<del>` element to correct a script:

> *... he travelled to Germany with his cousin,*
>   *<del>Charles Darwin</del>*
>   *<ins>Philip Sydney</ins>, who joined the embassy ...*

Note also the use of the `<ins>` element (see page 77) to show the replacement text.

The `<cite>` element

The `<cite>` element represents the title of a work (for example, the title of a book, an essay, a poem, a musical score, a song, a film, a TV show, a game, a sculpture, a painting, a theatrical production, an exhibition etc.)

A person's name is not the title of a work and the `<cite>` element must, therefore, not be used to mark up people's names.

Here is an example:

Brigadier-General **Samuel Arthur Einem Hickson** (C.B., D.S.O. R.E. Ret.) wrote the book *The Prince of Poets and Most Illustrious of Philosophers* which disputes the authenticity of **William Shakespeare** as the real author of the works attributed to him and claims that they were written by Sir **Francis Bacon**. He subtitled the book *What's in a Name!*.

The correct markup for this would be:

```
<p>Brigadier-General <b>Samuel Arthur Einem Hickson</b>
(C.B., D.S.O. R.E. Ret.)
wrote the book <cite>The Prince of Poets and Most Illustrious of
Philosophers</cite> which disputes the authenticity of <b>William
Shakespeare</b> as the real author of the works attributed to him and
claims that they were written by Sir <b>Francis Bacon</b>.
He subtitled the book <cite>What's in a Name!</cite>.</p>
```

Only global attributes may be used for the `<cite>` element.

A citation is *not* a quote for which the following element (the `<q>` element) should be used.

The `<q>` element

The `<q>` element should only be used for quotations. It is not intended to replace quotation marks for words or phrases which are not quotations. The use of `<q>` elements to mark up quotations is entirely optional, using explicit quotation punctuation without `<q>` elements is just as correct.

Example which incorporates both the `<cite>` element and the `<q>` element:

```
<p>Caroline Halstead writes in <cite>Life of Margaret Beaufort</cite>,
<q>The genius of literature hovered round the great-granddaughter
of the friend of Chaucer</q>, and she married Edmund Tudor.</p>
```

The `<dfn>` element

This is used to define a term, for example "LNER".

The *LNER* was a private company which ran trains from London to the North and East of the country. It was the second largest of the railway companies created by the *Railways Act* in 1923.

Running your cursor over the abbreviation "LNER" on a web page would give you the definition of the abbreviation.

The markup for the above is as follows:

```
<p>The <dfn><abbr title="London North Eastern Railway">LNER
</abbr></dfn> was a private company which ran trains from London
to the North and East of the country.
It was the second largest of the railway companies created by
the <i>Railways Act</i> in 1923.</p>
```

If the `<dfn>` element has a `title` attribute, then the value of that attribute is the term which must be defined.

Q. Why would one want to define a term? How could you use it?

If I were to write:

The Business Continuity Institute (BCI)

should I mark it up as

```
<dfn>The Business Continuity Institute (<abbr title="The Business Continuity
    Institute">BCI</abbr>)</dfn>
```

or

```
The Business Continuity Institute (<dfn><abbr title="The Business Continuity
    Institute">BCI</abbr></dfn>
```

?

A.

The former is correct if you are defining what the BCI is. The latter is correct if you are defining what the acronym "BCI" stands for, but not necessarily what it is.

The `<abbr>` element

The `<abbr>` element could be used to display someone's name from his initials

Example:

SAEH was the author of the book *The Prince of Poets*.

SAEH argued that Shakespeare was not well enough educated to have been able to write the plays attributed to him.

The markup is:

```
<p><dfn><abbr title="Samuel Arthur Einem Hickson">SAEH</abbr></dfn>
was the author of the book <cite>The Prince of Poets</cite>.</p>
<p><abbr title="Samuel Arthur Einem Hickson">SAEH</abbr>
argued that Shakespeare was not well enough educated to have been able
to write the plays attributed to him.</p>
```

- Attributes for the `<abbr>` element:
  - global attributes
  - including the `title` attribute which must and must only provide an expansion of the abbreviation

It can be seen that using the `<dfn>` and the `<abbr>` elements together, we can define an abbreviation in the first paragraph and then just use the abbreviation in subsequent sentences and paragraphs. However using the `<abbr>` element each time the abbreviation occurs in subsequent parts of the text enables the reader to hover over the abbreviation with a mouse if (s)he has forgotten the definition without having to go back through the text.

The `<ruby>` element

The `<ruby>` element allows one or more spans of phrasing content to be marked with ruby annotations, that is small annotations that can be placed above (or to the right) of a normal sized character or text.

Ruby annotations are normally or primarily used in East Asian typography as a guide for pronunciation or to include other annotations.

Only global attributes may be used for the `<ruby>` element.

The `<rt>` element

This conatins the annotation

The `<rp>` element

This should be used to display a text in case the browser does not support the `<ruby>` element. It should contain an explanation of what the user should be expected to see.

The `<rt>` and `<rp>` elements are used with the `<ruby>` element.

For example, consider the base word as "underneath" and the annotation as "over":

over
underneath

The markup is:

<ruby> underneath <rt>over</rt> </ruby>

another example, using other characters:

汉

The markup is:

<ruby> 汉 <rt>✍</rt> </ruby>

correctly, using the `<rp>` element, for a non supportive browser, such as Firefox, it would show:

汉 ✍ This browser does not support the `<ruby>` element, the symbol ✍ should appear as a very small character, centrally over the character 汉

Only global attributes may be used for these two elements.

The `<data>` element

This element is useful if you wish to be able to use the data in a table in another program (in a machine readable manner). Humans can see the values in the table, for example numbers spelt out, whilst a program can read the same numbers as figures (the data value).

Many documents show whole numbers from zero to nine as words and from ten upwards as numerals. Some even show numbers with two words, like ninety nine, as words, however convention has it that years are usually written as figures (2014).

When the attribute `value`, which must always be present, is date or time related, the more specific `time` element (see page 60) can be used instead.

Below is an example of stamps bought by post at a stamp auction:

Year	Nominal value	Cost + postage
1841	1d red	£26 + 97p
1902	7d grey	£3.75 + £1
1949	3d violet	40p + 75p

The markup would be:

```
<table sortable>
<thead> <tr> <th sorted>Year</th> <th>Nominal value</th>
        <th>Cost + postage</th> </tr> </thead>
<tbody>
<tr> <td>1841</td> <td> <data value="1">1d red</data></td>
     <td> <data value="2697">£26 + 97p</data></td> </tr>
<tr> <td>1902</td> <td> <data value="7">7d grey</data></td>
     <td> <data value="475">£3.75 + £1</data></td> </tr>
<tr> <td>1949</td> <td> <data value="3">3d violet</data></td>
     <td> <data value="115">40p + 75p</data></td> </tr>
</tbody>
</table>
```

Notes:

1. *The correct markup for the £ sign is* `&pound;`, *but has been shown as above for simplification*

2. *At the time of writing the attribute* `sortable` *hasn't been implemented by any browser yet*
3. *The machine readable value for the third column is the sum of the two figures given, in this case in pence*

The `<time>` element

Dates and Times do not need to be marked up as such. They can be recorded simply as ordinary text, for example:

The bus leaves at 4pm or at 16:00 if you prefer to use the 24 hour clock

However if you do use the `<time>` element, then it must represent a precise date and/or time using the Gregorian calendar.

The reason is that if used it must be able to be coded in a machine readable manner such that it could be used mathematically, even if it is not so intended.

For example:

The conference will start on October 5 and finish on the 20th.

which would be marked up as:

```
<p>The conference will start on
   <time datetime="2009-10-05">October 5</time>
   and finish on <time datetime="2009-10-20">the 20th</time>.</p>
```

Below are listed various acceptable syntaxes or strings which are valid for this element:

valid year string
   2014-11-18

valid month with year string
   2014-09

valid month without year string
   11-18

valid time string
   15:08

   15:08:39

15:08:39.528

valid date with time string
2014-09-18T15:08

2014-09-18T15:08:39

2014-09-18T15:08:39.528

2014-09-18 15:08

2014-09-18 15:08:39

2014-09-18 15:08:39.528

Only global attributes and the `datetime` attribute (see page 150) may be used with this element

The `<code>` element

The `<code>` element represents a fragment of computer code. This could be any string that a computer would recognize.

Example of part of a Pascal program:

```
<pre>
  <code>
    program test;
    var i: integer;
    begin
      i := 1;
    end.
  </code>
<pre>
```

Note that in order to retain the formatting I have added the element `<pre>` before and after the program.

Only global attributes may be used for the `<code>` element.

The `<var>` element

The `<var>` element represents a variable, for example:

The square on the hypotenuse is equal to the sum of the squares of the other two sides of a triangle (Pythagoras' theorem).

$$a^2 = b^2 + c^2$$

would be marked up as: (I have simplfied this by not showing the correct markup for the superscript ^{2})

`<var>`a`</var>`^{2} = `<var>`b`</var>`^{2} + `<var>`c`</var>`^{2}

The correct markup would be:

`<var>`a`</var>`² = `<var>`b`</var>`² + `<var>`c`</var>`²

One could argue that it would have been better to have used the language MathML for this markup, but that implies knowing that language.

Another example is: *There were `<var>`x`</var>` bottles of wine in my cellar today.*

Only global attributes may be used for the `<var>` element.

The `<sub>` element

The `<sub>` element represents a subscript

The `<sup>` element

and the `<sup>` element represents a superscript

Only global attributes may be used for the `<sub>` and `<sup>` elements.

Examples are:

The chemical formula for Water is H_2O, written

H₂O

$^7/_8$, or seven eighths could be written

⁷/₈

and a tenth could be written 10th, that is

10th

of course if detailed mathematical markup is desired then you could use the Mathematical Markup Language **MathML**

The translation for Miss in French is Mlle, written

Mlle

More correctly this should be:

<span lang="fr"><abbr>Mlle</abbr></span>

which leads us to:

The `<span>` element

The `<span>` element is rather like brackets, it enables you to use other attributes which could not be used on their own.

For example, if you wish to colour all the following text[7] *yellow* and you had written the appropriate code in a CSS file, then you could use the following:

Our Prince of poets, Shakespeare, whom we learn so early to love as our Romeo and Juliet's immortal throstle, returned home under his incognito of Francis Bacon in March 1579.

(if this book were in colour, the above text would have appeared in yellow, the colour I had chosen to show highlighting in the CSS file)

which could be marked up:

```
<p class="highlight">Our Prince of poets, Shakespeare, whom we learn so
            early to love as our Romeo and Juliet's immortal
            throstle, returned home under his incognito of Francis
            Bacon in March 1579.</p>
```

However if you only wanted to colour a few words of this text *yellow*, leaving the rest unchanged, then the attribute `class` needs a 'hook' to which it can be attached. `<span>` is such a hook, so we could write:

Our Prince of poets, Shakespeare, whom we learn so early to love as our Romeo and Juliet's immortal throstle, returned home under his incognito of Francis Bacon in March 1579.

(where only the words "immortal throstle" would have appeared in yellow)

The markup for this would be:

```
<p>Our Prince of poets, Shakespeare, whom we learn so
            early to love as our Romeo and Juliet's
            <span class="highlight">immortal
            throstle</span>, returned home under his incognito of Francis
            Bacon in March 1579.</p>
```

Only global attributes may be used for the `<span>` element.

---

7. Chapter XII from *The Prince of Poets*

The `<i>` element

The `<i>` element represents a span of text in an alternate voice or mood, or otherwise offset from the normal prose, such as a taxonomic designation, a technical term, an idiomatic phrase from another language, a thought, a ship's name, or some other prose whose typographical presentation is italicized.

The `<i>` element could be used where *typical typographic presentation* is expected to be italicized, but not if *stress* is intended, where `<em>` would be more appropriate.

Using the above sentence as an example, the markup would be:

> *`<p>`The `<code>`i`</code>` element could be used where `<i>`typical typographic presentation`</i>` is expected to be italicized, but not if `<em>`stress`</em>` is intended, where `<code>`em`</code>` would be more appropriate.`</p>`*

It should be noted that content in `<i>` or `<em>` elements will not necessarily be italicized as they have been here. Style sheets should be used to format them.

Only global attributes may be used for the `<i>` element.

The <b> element

The <b> element represents a span of text to be stylistically offset from the normal prose without conveying any extra importance, such as key words in a document abstract, product names in a review, or other spans of text whose typographical presentation is boldened.

The <b> element should be used as a last resort when no other element is more appropriate. In particular, headings should use the <h1> to <h6> elements, stress emphasis should use the <em> element, importance should be denoted with the <strong> element, and text marked or highlighted should use the <mark> element.

Example taken from an article on Frequency Distribution[8]:

<p>These curves are often referred to as <em>probability distributions</em> because the area bounded by the curve and specified, chosen, limits is equal to the probability of any value being between these limits. For instance the <b>probability</b> of picking a man at random from this group and who takes size 10 to 11 inclusive is 16 chances in 64, or 0.25.</p>

which would look like this:

"These curves are often referred to as *probability distributions* because the area bounded by the curve and specified, chosen, limits is equal to the probability of any value being between these limits. For instance the **probability** of picking a man at random from this group and who takes size 10 to 11 inclusive is 16 chances in 64, or 0.25."

Only global attributes may be used for the <b> element.

8. http://managers-net.org/frequencydistribution.html

The `<u>` element

The problem with the `<u>` element is that people are now used to seeing an underlined word or piece of text as a link to somewhere else, so it should be used sparingly. In many cases it may be more appropriate to use the `<em>` element. But see also the `<b>`, `<mark>`, `<cite>`, `<ruby>` and `<i>` elements

Suggested uses of this element are for labeling mispelt text or for proper names in Chinese text.

Example:

> When he wrote the leaflet he misspelt (sorry, mispelt) the destination. It should have been **Beijing**.

The markup is:

> *When he wrote the leaflet he mis<u>s</u>pelt (sorry, mispelt) the destination. It should have been Beijing.*

The `<mark>` element

When one does a search for a word or string of text, the search program usually `<mark>`s the search word or string.

Example, given the following text[9] (which includes some emphasized and some strong text) and the search string as *distribution*, the resultant text will look like this:

> *<p>It is important to note that where these frequency*
> *<mark>distribution</mark>s are used for estimating probability of events*
> *happening or not occurring, it is the area bounded by*
> *the curve and the limits chosen for the situation, and is not the*
> *height of the <mark>distribution</mark>.*
> *For example, referring to Figure 3 the <i>probability</i> that any man*
> *taken at random will be between 170 and 175 cm tall is the area bounded*
> *by the curve and the chosen limits of 170 and 175.*
> *From standard tables for the normal <mark>distribution</mark>, this*
> *area is approximately 34% or 0.34 of the whole area under the curve*
> *from left to right so the probability of this is 0.34.*
> *The actual number of men is 34% of 50,000 men or 17,000*
> *approximately.*
> *The probability that any man at random will be smaller than 170 cm will*
> *be 50% - 34% = 16% approximately.</p>*

which might be rendered thus:

> It is important to note that where these frequency distributions are used for estimating probability of events happening or not occurring, it is the **area** bounded by the curve and the limits chosen for the situation, and is **not the height** of the distribution. For example, referring to Figure 3 the *probability* that any man taken at random will be between 170 and 175 cm tall is the area bounded by the curve and the chosen limits of 170 and 175. From standard tables for the normal distribution, this area is approximately 34% or 0.34 of the whole area under the curve from left to right so the probability of this is 0.34. The *actual number* of men is 34% of 50,000 men or 17,000 approximately. The probability that any man at random will be smaller than 170 cm will be 50% - 34% = 16% approximately.

The `<mark>` element is used to bring particular attention to a particular part of a text or quotation which was not originally considered important in the original context.

Another example would be when a critic wanted to highlight some part of a speech or a spell or grammar checker wishes to highlight errors.

9. http://managers-net.org/frequencydistribution.html

For example:

"The perfectly
happy men," says Plutarch in effect, in writing for
children, "are those who can combine service to the
the state with the individual pursuit of Philosophy.
...,,10
...

(notice the two "the"s)

would be marked up thus:

<p><q>The perfectly
happy men,</q> says Plutarch in effect, in writing for
children, <q>are those who can combine service to <mark>the
the</mark> state with the individual pursuit of Philosophy.
... </q><span class="endnote">Adamson, <cite>Short History
of Education</cite>.</p>

Only global attributes may be used for the `<mark>` element.

10. Adamson, *Short History of Education.*

The `<br>` element

The `<br>` element represents a line break and should only be used when required by the normal context, for example in poems and in addresses. A stylesheet may modify this element causing line breaks to be rendered in a different way, for instance as green dots, or as extra spacing. It should be written `<br>`. Note that `</br>` and `<br/>` are incorrect.

This element does not have an end tag, it is a standalone element, although it may use global attributes.

Example[11]

> `<p>His life was gentle, and the elements<br>`
> `So mixed in him that Nature might stand up<br>`
> `And say to all the world, 'This was a man.'</p>`

Only global attributes may be used for the `<br>` element.

It would be **incorrect** to use the `<br>` element in this type of context:

> `<p>Saturday. Club event not to be missed<br>`
> `Sunday. Club dinner</p>`

which renders as:

> Saturday. Club event not to be missed
> Sunday. Club dinner

The correct manner would be to use a stylesheet to achieve the same result or to write:

> `<p>Saturday. Club event not to be missed</p>`
> `<p>Sunday. Club dinner</p>`

which renders as (without using a stylesheet):

> Saturday. Club event not to be missed
>
> Sunday. Club dinner

11. :Julius Caesar, Act V, sc v

The `<wbr>` element

The `<wbr>` element represents a line break **opportunity**.

For example, imagine a long line of text with no spaces between words:

SirNicholasBaconhadjustdiedandwelearnnothingofthewhereaboutsofLadyBaco
nbutthefollowingmonthhewrotealettertoGabrielHarveyfromLeicesterHousetheS
trandhouseoftheEarlwhereasaPrinceandtheEarl'ssonweshouldnaturallyexpecttof
indhim.

We can let the computer choose an intelligent line break, for example:

SirNicholasBaconhadjustdiedandwelearnnothingofthewhereaboutsof
LadyBaconbutthefollowingmonthhewrotealettertoGabrielHarveyfromLeicesterHouse
theStrandhouseofthe
EarlwhereasaPrinceandtheEarl'ssonweshouldnaturallyexpecttofindhim.

The markup for this example is:

*<p>SirNicholasBaconhadjustdiedandwelearnnothingofthewhereabout
sof<wbr>LadyBaconbutthefollowingmonthhewrotealetterto<wbr>Gab
rielHarvey<wbr>from<wbr>LeicesterHouse<wbr>theStrandhouse
<wbr>ofthe<wbr>EarlwhereasaPrinceandtheEarl'ssonweshouldnatur
allyexpecttofindhim.</p>*

It can also be used to break long lines of code in a program

Note that there is no end tag for the `<wbr>` element.

The `<samp>` element

This represents *output* from a computer. It is used mainly to style text.

The word "samp" itself could be considered to stand for "sample text"

Let's assume you are writing a computer text game. You wish to give the player several options like "take lead pipe" or "take spanner" or "take candlestick"

You could write:

Now choose your object: select `Take lead pipe` or `spanner` or `candlestick`

For which the markup would be:

```
<p>Now choose your object: select <samp>Take lead pipe</samp>
or <samp>spanner</samp> or <samp>candlestick</samp></p>
```

See also the `<code>`.

It could also be used, for example, to issue an error message:

`File not found` - The file you requested does not exist on this server.

For which the markup would be:

```
<p><samp>File not found</samp> - The file you requested does not exist on this server.</p>
```

Only global attributes may be used for the `<samp>` element.

The `<kbd>` element

This represents user *input* to a computer

Examples:

To make George eat an apple, press `Shift+F3`

To make George eat an apple, select `File|Eat Apple...`

and the markup is:

```
<p>To make George eat an apple, press <kbd>Shift+F3</kbd></p>
<p>To make George eat an apple, select <kbd>File|Eat Apple...</kbd></p>
```

Another example is:

To exit this program, if all else fails, Press `CTRL + ALT + DEL`

which would be marked up as:

```
<p>To exit this program, if all else fails,
Press <kbd>CTRL + ALT + DEL</kbd></p>
```

More correctly it should be written as:

```
<p>To exit this program, if all else fails,
Press <kbd>CTRL</kbd> + <kbd>ALT</kbd> + <kbd>DEL</kbd></p>
```

since the "+" is not part of the input (either keyboard or voice)

Only global attributes may be used for the `<kbd>` element.

The `<bdi>` element

bdi stands for Bi-directional Isolation. The clue is in the word 'Isolation'.

This element is intended for languages like Arabic, Hebrew, Persian, Thaana, Urdu, Kurcish and Yiddish which are written left to right. It will also work with any language like Chinese, Japanese, Korean, Thai and indeed English.

The intention is to keep all the characters of a word or phrase, written in any language, together irrespective of any other actions from a computer program. Many computer programs fail to display bidirectional text correctly. `<bdi>` acts like a block which the computer cannot alter.

It is difficult to give an example although some can be found on the internet, however 'בּבּ אֹ' would be written exactly as shown, (בּבּ אֹ) once this element has been implented in the browsers. Very few browsers support this element at the time of writing.

But see also the `<bdo>` element.

The `<bdo>` element

The `<bdo>` element represents explicit text directionality formatting control for its children. It allows authors to override the Unicode Bidirectional algorithm by explicitly specifying a direction override.

The `dir` attribute must be specified with its value set to either 'ltr' or 'rtl'. 'ltr' indicates that the text should be read **left to right** and 'rtl' indicates that the text should be read **right to left**.

For example English language text would be read left to right and arabic language text would be read right to left.

Example:

?siht daer uoy naC

and the markup:

```
<p><bdo dir="rtl">Can you read this?</bdo></p>
```

- Attributes for the `<bdo>` element:
  - global attributes
  - and the `dir` attribute set either to "ltr" or "rtl"

Editing a document

Once a document has been published and people have started to read it, they might be disturbed to find that it was later changed.

To be able to document these changes there are two elements which can be used, they are `<ins>` for additions to the document and `<del>` for deletions to the document. These elements must not cross paragraph (or even implied paragraph) boundaries and can only be used with two attributes `cite` and `datetime`.

Example. (The CSS stylesheet has been modified to show text with a line through it for deleted content, inserted content is automatically underlined.)

It was a lovely day on ~~Monday~~ <u>Wednesday</u>, but on Thursday it snowed. <u>I went skiing</u>

Here is the markup:

```
<p>It was a lovely day on <del>Monday</del> <ins>Wednesday</ins>,
    but on Thursday it snowed. <ins>I went skiing</ins></p>
```

To show when an edit was done the attribute `datetime` can be used.

Example:

```
<p class="markup">It was a lovely day on
    <del datetime="2014-01-05T15:20Z">Monday</del>
    <ins datetime="2014-01-05T15:20Z">Wednesday</ins>, but on Thursday it snowed.
    <ins datetime="2014-01-05T15:20Z">I went skiing</ins></p>
```

These datetimes are for the authors use, the reader would not see them.

Embedded content

- `<picture>`
- `<source>` when used with the `<picture>` element
- `<img>`
- `<iframe>`
- `<embed>`
- `<object>`
- `<param>`
- `<video>`
- `<audio>`
- `<source>`
- `<track>`
- `<media elements>`
- `<map>`
- `<area>`

The `<picture>` element

In order to display a picture for its best effect and as quickly as possible on your browsing equipment you need a picture with the best resolution for that equipment. A picture or image which fits well and displays a high quality or higher resolution display on your 19 inch monitor might not be the best you can get for your 3 inch smartphone. The `<picture>` element was designed to overcome this problem. If you only have one image then the conventional `<img>` element is the one to use, however if you are able to obtain (or make) two or more images at different resolutions then the html software can choose and display the best picture depending on the browsing equipment your reader is using. If you had a picture of a friend standing in a field with beautiful scenery, then on a desktop computer your reader could probably identify the person and appreciate the scenery, however on your mobile phone the friend would look like an ant in a field. So one of the alternative pictures might be just a close up of your friend. Here is an example of the markup you could use if you had three images, one suitable for a desktop monitor, one for an 8 inch tablet and one for a phone:

```
<picture>
<source media="(min-width: 45em)" srcset="manor_house.jpg">
<source media="(min-width: 30em)" srcset="fred_at_the_manor_house.jpg">
<source src="phone.jpg">
<img src="fallback.jpg" alt="This picture loads on non-supporting browsers">
</picture>
```

The user-agent, that's your browser, will choose the appropriate image from the three offered which is most suitable for the reader's or viewer's apparatus, but if the reader is using an older browser, the image chosen will be the one mentioned as "fallback" for the `<img>` element's `scr` attribute.

The `<picture>` element must always include one, and one only, `<img>` element.

This element can use global attributes, but see the `<source>` element which follows.

The `<source>` element when used with the `<picture>` element.

The `srcset` attribute must always be present, whilst the others are optional.

`srcset` stands for the source sets for the `<img>` element and it is this element which will display the ultimate image, the image which is chosen by the user agent (the browser) to be the most suitable for the equipment being used to view a page.

So we could write (within the `<picture>` element):

```
<source srcset="manor_house.jpg">
```

of course, it would be pointless to only give one image using the element `<picture>`, you could simply use `<img>` instead. So with multiple images you would need to indicate the suitable `media` as well. This is where the attributes `sizes` (see page 168) and `type` can be useful.

This element can be used with Global attributes as well as `srcset`, `sizes`, `media`, `type` attributes

The `<img>` element

The `<img>` element represents an image which is controlled by the `src` attribute

The `alt` attribute must also be present, even if it is an empty string, that is *alt=""*. This `alt` attribute is used by the browser only if it is unable to find the image for whatever reason, thus its contents (some text) should describe what the viewer would be expected to have seen and it is good practice to make the text flow as if the image were not there. The empty string should only be used if, in the absence of the image, it would be redundant to display anything else.

Although it is permitted to use dimension attributes (width, height), these are not recommended. If the aim is to change the size of the image this is much better done prior to the markup by using an image editor such as *The Gimp*. Failure to do this can (1) make the time taken to load the image much longer and (2) permit, usually by mistake, distortion of the image.

This element does not have an end tag, that is it finishes with the > character. It must have at least two attributes before the >

Example:

```
<figure>
 <img src=
 "http://www.traveldevel.org/hotel/iliessa hotel photos
        /viewofhotel/IMG_9204_300.jpg"
 alt="which is built from logs and has a swimming pool">
 <figcaption>I just wanted to tell you about this new
        hotel that I visited in Greece.</figcaption>
</figure>
```

which would be rendered as:

I just wanted to tell you about this new hotel that I visited in Greece.

The `<iframe>` element

The `<iframe>` element defines an inline frame that contains another document

For example:

<iframe seamless src="other_document.asp" width="300" height="200">
<p>Your browser doesn't appear to support iframes</p>
</iframe>

and if the following diagram is the file 'other_document.asp' then the result would be:

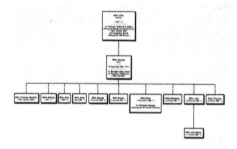

Other attributes that may be used with this element are: sandbox, seamless, name, srcdoc, allowfullscreen, width and height. The sandbox attribute can be used to disable many potential annoyances and the seamless attribute, if specified, makes it appear as part of the containing document

The attributes:

src
> This specifies the HTML file to be used

srcdoc
> This contains the HTML content of the page to use. If this is specified, and the browser supports it, then this overrules the src attribute.

sandbox
> Security rules for the nested content. Used on its own all the following are disallowed, however to lift any of them, the following tokens can be used:
> * *allow-same-origin*: Instead of the embedded content being from a unique (server or domain) origin, it is treated as being from its normal origin

- *allow-forms*: Allows the embedded browsing context to submit forms
- *allow-top-navigation*: Allows the embedded browsing context to navigate content to the top-level browsing context
- *allow-popups*: Allows popups
- *allow-scripts*: Permits scripts to be run
- *allow-printer-lock*: Allows the use of "Pointer Lock API"

Be careful when using any of these tokens. They potentially weaken the security of your website leaving it open to harmful attacks. Setting both the *allow-scripts* and *allow-same-origin* keywords together when the embedded page has the same origin (domain) as the page containing the `<iframe>` allows the embedded page to simply remove the `sandbox` attribute and then reload itself, effectively breaking out of the sandbox altogether.

`seamless`

makes the inline frame (iframe) appear to be part of the containing document by applying the document's styles to the nested content, for example by changing the fonts to those used in the containing document. It is a boolean attribute, present it is TRUE, absent it is FALSE.

`name`

The name of the iframe (text)

`allowfullscreen`

A boolean attribute, if present it allows the viewer to view the contents of the iframe in full screen. The default is FALSE.

`width`

allows the author to define the width of the iframe in pixels, e.g. width="200"

`height`

allows the author to define the height of the iframe in pixels, e.g. height="400"

The `seamless` attribute on the `<iframe>` element is not supported by many browsers yet.

The `<embed>` element

The `<embed>` element is typically used to run another application within the web page, for example a 'youtube' film or your own mp3 film.

```
<embed src="/actionwork4.mp3" type="video/quicktime"
        width="300" height="300">
```

Attributes:

- `src` - The address of the resource
- `type` - This is the type of the resource, for example, video/quicktime and audio/wav
- `width` - e.g. width="300" (in pixels)
- `height` - e.g. height="300" (in pixels)

This element does not have an end tag, that is it finishes with the > character. Of course it has one or more attributes before the >

The `<object>` element

The `<object>` element is similar to the `<embed>` element but can be used for html files, that is you can embed another html webpage into this html document. The `<embed>` element is more suitable for video type applications, but for images, use the `<img>` element.

```
<figure>
<legend>My trip</legend>
<object data="Travel4.html" width="200" height="150">
    File not found</object>
</figure>
```

Attributes:

- `data` - The address of the resource.
- `type` - This is the type of the resource, for example, pdf, video/ quicktime and audio/wav.
- `typemustmatch` - Whether the `type` matches the resource. If this object is used to reference resources from another domain, it is recommended to use this attribute.
- `name` - Any name.
- `usemap` - The image map to use.
- `form` - Associates the control with a `<form>`.
- `width` - e.g. width="300" (in pixels)
- `height` - e.g. height="300" (in pixels)

and, of course, global attributes

The <param> element

The <param> element is a child of an <object> element. That means that by using the <param> element various parameters may be passed to the <object> element before execution takes place.

<Param> elements must use both the name and the value attributes and these attributes can take any value, for example:

```
<figure>
<legend>My trip</legend>
<object data="Travel4.html" width="200" height="150">
 <param name="bgcolor" value="FFFFFF">
  File not found
</object>
</figure>
```

This element does not have an end tag, that is it finishes with the > character. Of course it has one or more attributes before the >

The `<video>` element

The `<video>` element represents a video or a movie.

Video formats available at the moment are: Ogg (Ogg Theora), mp4 and WebM (VP8). If these are not available then it is recommended that you use the `<object>` element.

Methods such as 'play', 'pause' and 'stop' map on to JavaScript methods.

Example:

1. Embed the video, add the controls (play, pause and stop) and choose the correct size for the screen:

```
<video src="firefox.ogg" controls width="300" height="200">
    The video wasn't found</video>
```

2. Make it autoplay, that is make it start playing as soon as it is loaded:

```
<video src="firefox.ogg" autoplay controls
    width="300" height="200">
    The video wasn't found</video>
```

3. We can also do this using JavaScript, so let us remove 'controls' but add some script:

```
<video src="firefox.ogg" autoplay width="300" height="200">
    The video wasn't found</video>
<script> var video = document.getElementsByTagName('video')[0];
</script>
<p>
  <input type=button value="&#x25FC;"
       onclick="video.pause();">
  <input type=button value="&#x25B6;"
       onclick="video.play();">
</p>
```

4. We could replace the buttons with one button:

```
<video src="firefox.ogg" autoplay width="300" height="200">
    The video wasn't found</video>
<script> var video = document.getElementsByTagName('video')[0];
</script>
<p>
  <input type=button value="&#x2588; &#x2588;"
```

```
    onclick="if (video.paused) video.play(); else video.pause();">
</p>
```

Note that the button value = ▶ shows an arrowhead ▶ for 'play' and the button value = ◼ shows a square for 'pause'. █ █ is another way of showing a 'pause' button. ■ ▮

However, using the `<source>` element one can overcome the problem of the different video formats. Rather than specifying the video source using the `src` attribute, one can nest multiple tags within the `<video>` element, each with a different video source enabling the browser to choose one which will work, or at least, the first which will play.

Example:

```
<video autoplay controls
    width="300" height="200">
    <source src="travel.ogg" type="video/ogg">
    <source src="travel.mp4" type="video/mp4">
    <source src="travel.webm" type="video/webm">
    The video wasn't found</video>
```

- Attributes for the `<video>` element:
    - global attributes
    - `src` - The address of the resource
    - `autoplay` - Start the video as soon as it is loaded
    - `loop` - If present, loop the video
    - `muted` - If present, mute the sound
    - `controls` - Show the controls (buttons)
    - `crossorigin` - How the element handles cross origin requests (see page 150)
    - `poster` - The poster or display to show before the video is played. This should give the address of an image file, it could even be an advertisement
    - `preload` - An indication of how much buffering the media resources might need
    - `mediagroup` - groups media elements together
    - `width` - e.g. width="300" (in pixels)
    - `height` - e.g. height="300" (in pixels)

The `<audio>` element

The `<audio>` element represents a sound or audio stream and is otherwise similar to the `<video>` element.

Audio formats supported at the moment are: Ogg (Vorbis), mp3 (mpeg) and Wav.

- Attributes for the `<audio>` element:
    - global attributes
    - `src` - The address of the resource
    - `autoplay` - Play it as soon as it is loaded
    - `loop` - If present, loop the audio
    - `muted` - If present, mute it
    - `controls` - Show the controls (buttons)
    - `preload` - An indication of how much buffering the media resources might need
    - `mediagroup` - groups media elements together
    - `crossorigin` - How the element handles cross origin (external resource) requests (see page 150)

look also at the `<track>` element (see page 91).

and the markup for a simple control bar:

```
<audio src="foobar.wav" controls preload="auto"></audio>
```

The `<source>` element

The `<source>` element is used to specify multiple media resources for the `<video>` and `<audio>` elements.

This element does not represent anything on its own.

It does not have an end tag, that is it finishes with the > character. Of course it has one or more attributes before the >

Example:

```
<video controls>
 <source src="...ogg" type="video/ogg">
 <source src="...mov" type="video/quicktime">
 I'm sorry, your browser doesn't support HTML video.
</video>
```

Attributes: Global, `src` and `type`.

Look also at the `<track>` element (see page 91).

The `<track>` element

The `<track>` element allows authors to specify explicit external timed text tracks for media elements. It does not represent anything on its own.

Attributes for the `<audio>` element:

- global attributes
- `kind` - Specifies the kind of text track: 'subtitles'; 'captions'; 'descriptions'; 'chapters' and 'metadata'. if missing this defaults to 'subtitles'.
- `src` - The address of the resource which must be present.
- `srclang` - The language of the text track (see page 8).
- `label` - A title, visible to the user.
- `default` - Enable the track if no other text track is more suitable.

Example:

```
<video src="europe.webm">
<track src=europe_en.vtt kind=subtitles srclang=en label="English">
<track src=europe_en_hoh.vtt kind=captions srclang=en
                label="English for the Hard of Hearing">
<track src=europe_fr.vtt kind=subtitles srclang=fr label="Français">
<track src=europe_de.vtt kind=subtitles srclang=de label="Deutsch">
</video>
```

The `<map>` element

The `<map>` element is used to construct an interactive image on a web page in conjunction with the `<area>` element.

For example, below is a map of some of the counties of England. Each county, shown in a different colour (in the original), can be selected and will take you to a different web page for that county. The markup is shown below and the details of the `<area>` element are explained in the following section.

NOTE: For simplicity of readability I have taken the liberty to show the coordinates in pairs separated by spaces and new lines. It should be noted that this is incorrect and neither spaces nor new lines are permitted between the coordinates.

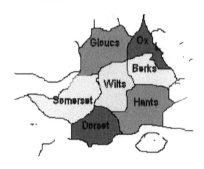

```
<p><img src="/ByCounty/WiltsMap.gif"
alt="Map of the counties around Wiltshire"
usemap="#counties"></p>
<map name="counties">
<area shape="poly"
   coords="109,80, 108,79, 87,79, 92,74,
       92,55, 89,50, 89,45, 107,28,
       107,19, 111,18, 121,18, 130,23,
       146,14, 150,14, 160,28, 164,29,
       157,43, 157,60, 150,63, 135,63,
       121,71, 117,77, 117,79"
   title="Gloucestershire"
   href="/ByCounty/Gloucestershire.html" alt="Gloucestershire">
<area shape="poly"
   coords="157,60, 157,43, 164,21, 179,5,
       191,30, 192,39, 206,51, 203,52,
       203,57, 217,72, 199,73, 194,65,
       194,61, 188,60, 191,56, 191,51, 180,51"
   title="Oxfordshire"
   href="/ByCounty/Oxfordshire.html" alt="Oxfordshire">
<area shape="poly"
```

```
    coords="157,60, 191,51, 191,56, 188,60, 194,61,
        194,65, 199,73, 217,72, 222,79, 225,87,
        213,99, 206,95, 191,93, 167,93, 165,90,
        164,85, 158,80, 157,75"
    title="Berkshire"
    href="/ByCounty/BerkshireLocations.html" alt="Berkshire">

  <area shape="poly"
    coords="117,79, 117,77, 121,71, 135,63, 150,63, 157,60,
        157,75, 158,80, 164,85, 165,90, 167,93, 162,100,
        158,100, 155,102, 156,109, 156,124, 153,129, 136,130,
        131,126, 126,123, 111,121, 112,118, 114,114, 116,112,
        121,104, 117,89, 114,89, 114,85, 118,85"
    title="Wiltshire"
    href="/ByCounty/Wiltshire2.html" alt="Wiltshire">

  <area shape="poly"
    coords="136,130, 153,129, 156,124, 156,109, 155,102, 158,100,
        162,100, 167,93, 191,93, 206,95, 213,99, 214,112,
        222,117, 206,130, 206,149, 190,147, 176,146, 172,152,
        172,155, 170,157, 163,160, 150,160, 150,156, 147,155,
        145,143, 145,139, 137,132"
    title="Hampshire"
    href="/ByCounty/Hampshire.html" alt="Hampshire">
  <area shape="poly"
    coords="136,130, 137,132, 145,139, 145,143, 147,155, 150,156,
        150,160, 144,160, 141,160, 137,165, 137,169, 131,174,
        117,173, 109,172, 107,177, 103,177, 100,169, 91,166
        79,166, 79,146, 103,132, 106,132, 111,125, 111,121,
        126,123, 131,126"
    title="Dorset"
    href="/ByCounty/Dorset.html" alt="Dorset">
  <area shape="poly"
    coords="111,121, 111,125, 106,132, 103,132, 79,146, 76,142,
        67,138, 57,138, 48,137, 42,134, 17,107, 32,106,
        41,107, 48,113, 61,112, 62,106, 68,100, 75,99,
        78,92, 82,89, 81,85, 87,79, 108,79, 109,80,
        117,79, 118,85, 114,85, 114,89, 117,89, 121,104,
        116,112, 114,114, 112,118"
    title="Somerset"
    href="/ByCounty/Somerset.html" alt="Somerset">
</map>
```

The `<area>` element

The `<area>` element defines the area of any shape enclosed within its borders. It is defined by the coordinates (the `coords` attribute) of the shape. The shape can be a circle, a polygon or a rectangle. If no `coords` attribute is present then it is the area of the whole image. The `href` attribute represents a hyperlink.

This element does not have an end tag, that is it finishes with the > character. Of course it has several attributes before the > so we get:

<area attribute="whatever" another_attribute="something else">

Attributes for the `<area>` element:

- global attributes
- `alt` - Replacement text when images are not available. Should describe the image.
- `coords` - The coordinates for the shape to be created.
- `shape` - The kind of shape, e.g. 'circle', rectangle ('rect'), polygon ('poly').
- `href` - the URL address
- `target` - '_blank' = new window; '_self' = same window; '_parent' = opens in the parent frameset; '_top' = full body of the window.
- `download` - whether to download the resource. Add the filename. This is not supported in every browser.
- `ping` - URLs to ping.
- `rel` - specifies the relationship between the current document and the target URL
- `hreflang` - The language of the resource.
- `type` - specifies the type of the URL

Interactive elements

- The `<details>` element
- The `<summary>` element
- The `<menu>` element
- The `<menuitem>` element
- The `<dialog>` element

The `<details>` element

The `<details>` element represents further information that might not be shown by default which the user can obtain on demand.

It is *not* appropriate for footnotes.

The `open` attribute indicates that the details are to be shown to the user. If absent only the summary is shown.

Example of the markup:

```
<details>
<summary>The Book of Hicksons</summary>
<p>The Genealogy of the Hickson, Hixon, Hixson and Higson families
  from the Domesday Book to about 1600.</p>
</details>
```

The resulting display would be:

The Book of Hicksons

However, if the attribute `open` were inserted (*<details open>*) the viewer would see:

The Book of Hicksons

The Genealogy of the Hickson, Hixon, Hixson and Higson families from the Domesday Book to about 1600.

The `<details>` element is not supported properly by all browsers yet.

The `<summary>` element

The `<summary>` element represents a summary, a caption or a legend for the rest of the contents of the `<summary>` element's parent, the `<details>` element, if any.

For an example see the `<details>` element.

The `<menu>` element

The `<menu>` element represents a list of commands. There are two different `type`s: toolbar and popup. A menu can call another menu.

Commands can be activated using the `<a>` element together with the `href` attribute or by means of radio buttons, checkboxes or an access key like `Shift | Control | F3`. Commands can also be disabled and can appear as greyed out or even hidden.

type=Toolbar

○details | ○summary | ○menu | ○menuitem

and the markup:

```
<menu>
  <li><input type="radio" name="Interactive_elements">details</li>
  <li><input type="radio" name="Interactive_elements">summary</li>
  <li><input type="radio" name="Interactive_elements">menu</li>
  <li><input type="radio" name="Interactive_elements">menuitem</li>
</menu>
```

type=Popup

```
<menu>
 <li>
  <button type="menu" value="Techniques" menu="filemenu">
  <menu type="popup" id="filemenu">
    <menuitem label="Variance" onclick="rvar()">
    <menuitem label="Ergonomics" onclick="rerg()">
    <menuitem label="Heuristics" onclick="rheu()">
    <menuitem label="Synthesis" onclick="rsyn()">
  </menu>
 </li>
 <li>
  <button type="menu" value="Biographies" menu="filemenu">
  <menu type="popup" id="filemenu">
    <menuitem label="Bedaux" onclick="bbedaux()">
    <menuitem label="Currie" onclick="bcurrie()">
    <menuitem label="Gilbreth" onclick="bgilbreth()">
    <menuitem label="Taylor" onclick="btaylor()">
  </menu>
 </li>
 <li>
  <button type="menu" value="Case Studies" menu="filemenu">
```

```
<menu type="popup" id="filemenu">
    <menuitem label="Reduction" onclick="csred()">
    <menuitem label="Measuring" onclick="csmea()">
    <menuitem label="Improving" onclick="csimp()">
  </menu>
 </li>
</menu>
```

At the time of writing neither the `<menu>` element nor the `<menuitem>` element are supported by any browser, however when the are supported it should look like this, assuming that the first button had been activated:

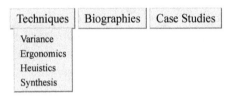

Attributes for the `<menu>` element:

- Global attributes
- `type` - type of menu
- `label` - a label for the menu which is used to display nested menus. To be used only if `type` is Popup

The `<menuitem>` element

This should be used with the `<menu>` element when the `type` is "popup".

Example

```
<button type=menu menu=editmenu>Commands...</button>
<menu type="popup" id="editmenu">
  <menuitem type="radio" radiogroup="alignment" checked="checked"
        label="Left" icon="icons/alL.png" onclick="setAlign('left')">
  <menuitem type="radio" radiogroup="alignment"
        label="Center" icon="icons/alC.png" onclick="setAlign('center')">
  <menuitem type="radio" radiogroup="alignment"
        label="Right" icon="icons/alR.png" onclick="setAlign('right')">
  <hr>
  <menuitem type="command" disabled
        label="Publish" icon="icons/pub.png" onclick="publish()">
</menu>
```

Attributes for the `<menuitem>` element:

- type - The type of command
- label - A user visible label
- icon - An icon for the command
- disabled - True or False for the form control
- checked - Whether the command or control id checked
- radiogroup - A name for the group of commands to be treated as a radio button group
- default - Mark the command as being a default command
- command - The definition of the command
- title - This gives a hint describing the command which might be shown to the user to help him/her

The `<dialog>` element

The `<dialog>` element enables users to create popup dialogs.

Example:

Note that the `<main>` should draw the user's attention to the more important parts of the dialogue as opposed to the smallprint.

Here is the markup:

```
<dialog open>
<h3>Lunch Time</h3>
<main>
 <p>Are you ready for lunch?</p>
</main>
 <p><small>If you don't come now, it will go cold.</small></p>
</dialog>
```

Without the attribute `open` the dialog would be hidden, this attribute makes it "popup" on top of the work you have on the screen.

The difference between the 3 elements `<nav>`, `<ul>` and `<menu>`

- The `<nav>` element is to help readers navigate between different areas of a website and uses the `<ul>` element together with the `<li>` element
- The `<menu>` element is to be used to enable commands to be issued as opposed to navigating between different places
- The `<ul>` element is specifically for lists of any type and should be used where the `<nav>` and the `<menu>` elements are not more appropriate

The `<menu>` element is not fully supported by browsers yet.

Tables

Tables exist for tabular data. Let's read part of Samuel Hickson's *The Prince of Poets*:

Chapter VII	Chapter VIII
Shakespeare in 1572	Shakespeare, princely pleasures
The muse of the yet youthful Shakespeare-Bacon, that most industrious of honey-bees, was now not only beginning to sing, but already eager that her voice should be heard.	Let the reader picture to himself an England, half of which was forestland full of game, with a Thames full of salmon; but no railways, no better roads than a cart track.

You follow this story easily, written in two columns of a table, because you can see it and you know that you have to read one column and then the next. But imagine that you are blind. You can get the computer to read it for you. Depending on the intelligence of the computer program, it may read from left to right, so you get

> Chapter seven Chapter eight Shakespeare in fifteen seventy two Shakespeare, princely pleasures

etc. It reads across, not in columns. There are many other types of media presentation, for example: graphical displays, television screens, handheld devices, speech-based browsers, braille-based tactile devices, etc. The same applies for pictures, for headers and for navigation aids (menus). Headers can be 'placed' logically by using the correct markup, that is `<h1>` for the main header; `<h2>` for the next level; `<h3>` for the next less important or sub level etc. (down to `<h6>`). Pictures or images can be placed on the left or the right or in the centre by using the appropriate style.

But if you want to present some information like the results for a race (Place, Name, Time, Category) or the results of some experiment (Type, Class 1, Class 2, Class3), *then* tables are the correct markup to use. Tables must not be used as layout aids. For that you should use CSS.

Below are the elements used for tables:

```
<table>
  <caption>...</caption> (optional, but only one)
  <colgroup>...</colgroup> (optional)
  <thead>...</thead> (optional, but only one)
  <tfoot>...</tfoot> (optional, but only one)
  <tbody> (optional)
    <tr>
      <th>...</th>
      <td>...</td>
    </tr>
  </tbody> (to close tbody)
</table>
```

Global attributes and the attribute sortable may be used for the <table> element.

The <caption> element

The <caption> element represents the title of the <table>. Should the <table> be part of a <figure> element then the <caption> element should be omitted in favour of the <legend>.

The <caption> may contain descriptive text in addition to the title.

Only global attributes may be used for the <caption> element.

The <colgroup> element

The <colgroup> element is used to group columns in a table for formatting. It is useful for applying styles to entire columns instead of repeating them for each cell.

The <col> element

The <col> element specifies attributes for an entire column, which avoids having to specify these attributes for each cell, and when used with the id tag can help to identify columns in a table

This element does not have an end tag, that is it finishes with the > character. Of course it has one or more attributes before the >

Example:

```
<table>
<col id="mcol1">
<col id="mcol2" bgcolor="red">
...
</table>
```

If used with the `span` attribute it can specify more than one column at a time.

The `<thead>` element

The purpose of the `<thead>` element is to give headings for each column in the table and if the table spans more than one page it is repeated at the top of each page when printed on paper.

`<thead>` element must come before any `<tfoot>`, `<tbody>` and `<tr>` elements. It is not permitted to have more than one `<thead>` element. It should contain one or more `<tr>` elements.

Inside this `<tr>` element only the `<th>` element is allowed. The `<td>` element is not allowed

Only global attributes may be used for the `<thead>` element.

The `<tfoot>` element

The `<tfoot>` element is intended for totals or comments which should appear underneath the table. Comments can span the entire row if used with the `colspan` attribute. However this element must be placed between the `<thead>` and `<tbody>` elements.

Only global attributes may be used for the `<tfoot>` element.

The `<tbody>` element

The `<tbody>` element may be used after any `<caption>`, `<colgroup>` and `<thead>` elements. It contains the matrix of rows and columns which are formed by `<tr>` elements.

Only global attributes may be used for the `<tbody>` element.

The `<tr>` element

The `<tr>` element represents a row of cells in a table and must contain `<th>` and / or `<td>` elements for it to display any data. There is no limit to the pairs of `<tr>`...`</tr>` elements in a table.

Only global attributes may be used for the `<tr>` element.

The `<th>` element

The `<th>` element represents a header cell in a table.

Attributes which may be used:

- Global
- colspan - The number of columns the cell spans
- rowspan - The number of rows the cell spans
- headers - The header cells for this cell
- scope - Specifies to which cell the header applies
- abbr - Alternative label to use for the header cell when referencing the cell in other contexts
- sorted - Column sort

The `<td>` element

The `<td>` element represents a data cell in a table.

Attributes which may be used:

- Global
- colspan - The number of columns the cell spans
- rowspan - The number of rows the cell spans
- headers - The header cells for this cell

Example of the use of a table:

Half Marathon Results			
Position	**Name**	**Time**	**PB**
28th	Chris Bryant	1:28:02	PB
29th	Peter Smith	1:28:04	PB
33rd	Steve Rington	1:28:56	
35th	Liz Atkinson	1:42:47	PB
114th	Ali Field	1:42:47	
221st	Joyce Roberts	2:01:49	
235th	Debbie Johnson	2:07:49	
PB means Personal Best			

Here is the markup:

```
<table>
<caption>Half Marathon Results</caption>
<thead>
 <tr>
  <th>Position</th>
  <th>Name</th>
  <th>Time</th>
  <th>PB</th>
 </tr>
</thead>
<tfoot>
 <tr>
  <td colspan=4>PB means Personal Best</td>
 </tr>
</tfoot>
<tbody>
 <tr>
  <td>28th</td>
  <td>Chris Bryant</td>
  <td>1:28:02</td>
  <td>PB</td>
 </tr>
 <tr>
  <td>29th</td>
  <td>Peter Smith</td>
  <td>1:28:04</td>
  <td>PB</td>
 </tr>
 <tr>
```

```
 <td>33rd</td>
 <td>Steve Rington</td>
 <td>1:28:56</td>
 <td></td>
</tr>
<tr>
 <td>35th</td>
 <td>Liz Atkinson</td>
 <td>1:42:47</td>
 <td>PB</td>
</tr>
<tr>
 <td>114th</td>
 <td>Ali Field</td>
 <td>1:42:47</td>
 <td></td>
</tr>
<tr>
 <td>221st</td>
 <td>Joyce Roberts</td>
 <td>2:01:49</td>
 <td></td>
</tr>
<tr>
 <td>235th</td>
 <td>Debbie Johnson</td>
 <td>2:07:49</td>
 <td></td>
</tr>
</tbody>
</table>
```

Forms

Forms allow interaction between the client (the person completing the form) and the server, they are also a means of enabling the client to submit information to (let's call him/her) the owner of the form. It can contain textfields, checkboxes, radio-buttons and more.

It should be noted that some HTML 4.01 attributes are no longer supported, but there are many new HTML attributes.

Let's start with an example and then explain it:

```
<form>
  <fieldset>
    <legend>The HTML 10k race series</legend>
```

The `<form>` element will have some attributes, probably something like:

```
<form
    name=...
    onSubmit=...
    method=...
    action=... >
```

but the attributes will be discussed later (see page 129).

The next two lines enable us to input the Surname and the First Name. The `<input>` element is discussed later (see page 113)

<p>Surname <input type="text" size="24" name="lastname" autocomplete="on">
First name <input type="text" size="24" name="firstname">

Next we need to see the radio control in action. The `<label>` element is discussed on page 113 but can be used for type=radio where only one selection can be made, that is there is a toggle action, or it can be used for type=checkbox where multiple selections are possible.

<label><input type=radio name=Sex> Male</label>
<label><input type=radio name=Sex> Female</label></p>

We will close this line (with </p>) and start the next to input the e-mail address, password and date of birth.

There is an attribute `disabled` which I am showing here, this attribute enables the web page writer to prevent the reader entering anything into this field whilst, nevertheless, having it available should you wish to reintroduce it. The type=email will check that the address entered contains the '@' symbol between two strings and helps the user to avoid mistakes when the field is enabled.

<p>E-mail address <input type=email disabled>

The type=password ensures that the text field is obscured probably with dots or asterisks:

<label>Password <input type=password required></label>

The date of birth can be entered from a drop down calendar. Just click on the arrow at the end of the field (only works in the browser Opera at the time of writing):

Date of birth <input type=Date size=10></p>

Next we need to choose which races, April, May, June, July or/and August in which the user wishes to participate, so we will use the `<select>` and

`<option>` elements. The reader may select one of more months by either clicking on one, or (using the Control key) by clicking on several.

```
<p><select multiple name="use">
   <option value="1">April race</option>
   <option value="2">May race</option>
   <option value="3">June race</option>
   <option value="4">July race</option>
   <option value="5">August race</option>
</select> Select those in which you would like to participate</p>
```

Now we need to choose in which category the reader should run. We need to show a list from which we can select a category and the `<datalist>` element is the most suitable:

Category

Clicking on the box or trying to enter a character brings down this list:

```
Junior
Senior
Veteran
Super Veteran
```

```
<p><label>Category <input list="agegroups"></label>
   <datalist id="agegroups">
     <option value="Junior"></option>
     <option value="Senior"></option>
     <option value="Veteran"></option>
     <option value="Super Veteran"></option>
   </datalist></p>
</fieldset>
```

Well! that's the personal details dealt with. It would be good to have a comments box. For this we use a simple `<textarea>` element. Although we can state the size of the box, this does not stop the user from entering more data than is visible.

```
<fieldset>
<legend>Anything else we should know?</legend>
 <p><textarea rows="2" cols="20" name="enquiries"></textarea></p>
</fieldset>
```

Finally we need to submit the data collected or let the user reset the whole form and start again.

```
<fieldset>
<legend>Submit or start again</legend>
 <p><button>Try it <input type=submit></button> - or -
```

```
<button>I made a mistake <input type=reset></button></p>
    </fieldset>
</form>
```

Below are listed the other elements necessary to capture the data for forms.

- `<fieldset>`
- `<label>`
- `<input>`
- `<button>`
- `<select>`
- `<datalist>`
- `<optgroup>`
- `<option>`
- `<textarea>`
- `<keygen>`
- `<output>`
- `<progress>`
- `<meter>`
- `<legend>`

The `<fieldset>` element

The `<fieldset>` element is used as a container to group together elements in forms.

For example, in a form you could request all the personal details of a client, then all their requirements followed by any comments they may wish to make. Each of these three groups could be in a fieldset.

Here is a partial example to show its use:

```
Personal details

Requirements

Comments
```

and the markup:

```
<form>
 <fieldset>
  <p>Personal details</p>
 </fieldset>
 <fieldset>
  <p>Requirements</p>
 </fieldset>
 <fieldset>
  <p>Comments</p>
 </fieldset>
</form>
```

Attributes:

- Global
- form
- name

The `<label>` element

The `<label>` element is used to define a caption for a control and if used for the type 'radio' then it will toggle the control.

It can be used like this:

```
<p>
 <label><input type="radio" name=Sex> Male</label>
 <label><input type="radio" name=Sex> Female</label>
</p>
```

or this, where the `for` attribute and the 'id' must have the same values, for example:

```
<p>
 <input type="radio" name=Sex id="male">
 <label for="male">Male</label>
 <input type="radio" name=Sex id="female">
 <label for="female">Female</label>
</p>
```

The resulting output should look like this whichever markup you use:

◯ Male ◯ Female

The `<input>` element

The `<input>` element represents a typed data field, usually with a form control to allow the user to edit the data.

The main attributes are `type` and `name` which will be discussed in detail in the attributes section. (see page 125) By default *input type="text"* is used which represents one line of text.

Surname [   ]

Below is the markup:

```
<p>
 <label>Surname</label>
 <input type="text" name="surname" size="20" maxlength="80">
</p>
```

This element does not have an end tag, that is it finishes with the > character. Of course it has one or more attributes before the >

The `<button>` element

The `<button>` element is used to submit or reset a `<form>`, for example:

Submit or Start again **Confirm booking** **Reset**

and the markup is:

```
<fieldset>
  <legend>Submit or Start again</legend>
    <button type="submit" name="send">Confirm booking</button>
    <button type="reset">Reset</button>
</fieldset>
```

The `<select>` element

The `<select>` element represents a control for selecting amongst a set of options, for example it is used to select an item from amongst a list of options.

Which was Shakespeare's first play? The Comedy of Errors ▼

and clicking on the arrowhead which should be shown on the right hand end will produce the drop down list of choices:

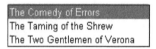

The markup is:

```
<fieldset>
<legend>Which was Shakespeare's first play?</legend>
<select>
  <option value="Errors">The Comedy of Errors</option>
  <option value="Shrew">The Taming of the Shrew</option>
  <option value="Gentlemen">The Two Gentlemen of Verona</option>
</select>
</fieldset>
```

The `<datalist>` element

This is another way of selecting data from a list, but in this case the list is hidden but can be viewed by starting to enter data into the `<input>` element which needs to be present. The datalist needs an `id` which must be the same as the attribute `list` for the `<input>` element.

Here is an example which uses two `<datalist>`s linked to two `<input>` boxes:

```
┌─Which was Shakespeare's first play and when was it written?───────────────────────────┐
│  ┌──────────────────┐ ┌──────────────────┐                                            │
│  └──────────────────┘ └──────────────────┘                                            │
└────────────────────────────────────────────────────────────────────────────────────────┘
```

... and the markup used:

```
<fieldset>
<legend>Which was Shakespeare's first play and when was it written?
</legend>
<input list="titles">
<input list="dates">
<datalist id="titles">
 <option value="The Comedy of Errors" label="1"></option>
 <option value="The Taming of the Shrew" label="2"></option>
 <option value="The Two Gentlemen of Verona" label="3"></option>
</datalist>
<datalist id="dates">
 <option value="1572 aged 11" label="A"></option>
 <option value="1584" label="B"></option>
 <option value="1591" label="C"></option>
 <option value="Some other date" label="D"></option>
</datalist>
</fieldset>
```

Note that each option has a `value` and a `label`.

Only global attributes may be used for the `<datalist>` element.

The `<optgroup>` element

The `<optgroup>` element enables you to `<select>` one item from within various groups, for example from plays by Shakespeare (with a list) to plays by Molière (with a list)

> Midsummer-Night's Dream
> Le Misanthrope

and clicking on the arrowhead which should be on the right hand end will produce the drop down list of choices:

The markup is:

```
<select>
 <optgroup label="Shakespeare">
  <option value="summer">Midsummer-Night's Dream</option>
  <option value="winter">The Winter's Tale</option>
  <option value="storm">The Tempest</option>
  <option value="wellwell">All's Well that Ends Well</option>
 </optgroup>
 <optgroup label="Moliere">
  <option value="misanthrope">Le Misanthrope</option>
  <option value="wives">L'école des femmes</option>
  <option value="hypocrite">Tartuffe ou l'Imposteur</option>
  <option value="hypocondriac">Le Malade imaginaire</option>
 </optgroup>
</select>
```

The text given as the `value` attribute can be anything. However it is used by the program (Perl, JavaScript or whatever) which has been named by the `action` attribute of the `<form>` element.

The `<option>` element

The `<option>` element is used with the `<select>`, `<datalist>` and `<optgroup>` elements. Its attributes are described later (see page 135). See the previous page for examples.

The `<textarea>` element

The `<textarea>` element represents a multiline area of text. Its visible size can be defined, but this does not prevent the user from entering as much text as (s)he pleases unless `maxlength` or `minlength` are used.

Enter any text here ...

and the markup:

```
<textarea rows="2" cols="30" placeholder="Enter any text here ..."></textarea>
```

Attributes for the `<textarea>` element:

- Global attributes
- `autocomplete` — Hint for form autofill feature
- `autofocus` — Automatically focus the form control when the page is loaded
- `cols` — Maximum number of characters per line
- `dirname` — Name of form field to use for sending the element's directionality in form submission
- `disabled` — Whether the form control is disabled
- `form` — Associates the control with a form element
- `inputmode` — Hint for selecting an input modality
- `maxlength` — Maximum length of value
- `minlength` — Minimum length of value
- `name` — Name of form control to use for form submission and in the form.elements API
- `placeholder` — User-visible label to be placed within the form control
- `readonly` — Whether to allow the value to be edited by the user
- `required` — Whether the control is required for form submission
- `rows` — Number of lines to show
- `wrap` — How the value of the form control is to be wrapped for form submission

The `<keygen>` element

The `<keygen>` element enables you to request identification with a certificate using private and public keys, that is, to authenticate users.

It does not have an end tag, that is it finishes with the > character.

Example:

and the markup:

```
<form action="processkey.cgi" method="post" enctype="multipart/form-data">
 <p><keygen name="your_key"></p>
 <p><input type=submit value="Submit your key ..."></p>
</form>
```

`<keygen>` is not supported by Microsoft and it seems very unlikely that it ever will be.

The `<output>` element

The `<output>` element represents the result of a calculation of 'form-associated' elements, notably by a script.

Example:

| 3.76 | + | 6.78 | = 10.54 |

The markup:

```
<form onsubmit="return false"
      oninput="n1.value = x1.valueAsNumber + y.valueAsNumber">
 <input name="x1" type="number" step=any> +
 <input name="y" type="number" step=any> =
 <output name="n1" for="x1 y"></output>Result
</form>
```

and another example using type=range:

Percentage ──────◯────── 50%

The markup:

```
<form onsubmit="return false" oninput="n2.value = x2.valueAsNumber">
<label for="x2">Percentage</label>
<input name="x2" type="range" step=10>
<output name="n2" for="x2"></output>50%
</form>
```

The `<progress>` element

The `<progress>` element represents the completion progress of a task. Its attributes are `value` and `max` as well as the global attributes. In its simplest form it could be written as:

```
<p>The progress is: <progress value="67" max="100"></p>
```

and the result would be:

The progress is: ▮▮▮▮▮▮▮▮▮▮

But it is unlikely that you would want to fix the progress, since progress would, hopefully, be always changing, so you would probably need to use a variable which was called from a script. for example:

The progress is: ▮▮

for which the markup would be:

```
<p>The progress is: <progress id="x" max="100"></p>
    <script>
    var progressing = document.getElementById('x');
    function updateProgress(update_x) {
        progressing.value = update_x;
        progressing.getElementsByTagName('s')[0].textContent = update_x; }
    </script>
```

However should you wish to represent a scalar measurement then the correct element would be:

The `<meter>` element

The `<meter>` element represents a scalar value in a specified range or a fractional value. As well as the global attributes, it can have up to six other attributes: `min`, `max`, `value`, `low`, `high` and `optimum`.

These examples are equivalent:

20%
3 apples out of 15 were bad
<meter min="0" max="100" value="20"></meter>

- the slider was green

... and the result for a non compatible browser would be:

"3 apples out of 15 were bad"

The markup is:

<meter min="0" max="100" value="20">3 apples out of 15 were bad</meter>

Here is an example of polling results:

The minimum number of votes 'myparty' could win is zero and the maximum, all the votes, is 27,000. Actually we won 18,947, of course the optimum would be all the votes. It would be a poor result if we only won 435 and an excellent result with 21,000.

- the slider was golden

... and the result for a non compatible browser would be:

"Seats gained by my party"

The colour, depending on the browser, is golden because of the use of the `optimum` attribute.

This is the markup:

<meter id="myparty" min="0" max="27000" value="18947"
optimum="27000" low="435" high="21000">
Seats gained by my party</meter>

Note that the comment "Seats gained by my party" would only appear if this element was not supported by the browser.

The `<legend>` element

The `<legend>` element defines a caption for the `<fieldset>`, `<figure>` or `<details>` elements, that is it gives a title to a list, a form or other things. It must be the first line of these elements, for example:

Your contact details
Surname

First name

Your e-mail:

The markup would be:

```
<fieldset>
  <legend>Your contact details</legend>
  <dl>
    <dt><label>Surname</label></dt>
    <dd><input type="text" name="pname" size="20"
      maxlength="40"></dd>

    <dt><label>First name</label></dt>
    <dd><input type="text" name="prenom" size="20"
      maxlength="80"></dd>

    <dt><label>Your e-mail:</label></dt>
    <dd><input type="text" name="email" size="40"
      maxlength="80"></dd>
  </dl>
</fieldset>
```

It can also be used (once only) within a `<figure>` element (see page 44).

Only global attributes may be used for the `<legend>` element.

The `<canvas>` element

The `<canvas>` element represents a resolution-dependent bitmap canvas which can be used for rendering graphs, game graphics, or other visual images on the fly. It uses JavaScript.

For example it could show a clockface always showing the correct time.

It is obviously impossible to give a working example on paper, but I would recommend the web site *https://labs.mininova.org/canvas/* which gives many examples.

An example which will draw a random line on your screen is given below:

```
<h1>Canvas demo</h1>
<canvas width="800" height="450"></canvas>
<script>
var context =
   document.getElementsByTagName('canvas')[0].getContext('2d');
context.beginPath();
context.moveTo(context.canvas.width * Math.random(),
   context.canvas.height * Math.random());
context.lineTo(context.canvas.width * Math.random(),
   context.canvas.height * Math.random());
context.stroke();
</script>
```

By default the size of a `<canvas>` is 300px x 150px. To change this use the attributes `width` and `height` as seen above.

It now has lots of different features, but at the time of writing, `<canvas>` only works in four different browsers, Safari which is the operating system used by the Mac, Opera, Firefox and Google's Chrome. It has not yet been implemented by Microsoft.

For a more detailed description of the element `<canvas>` (see page 175).

Drag and Drop

An interface which can be added to your web page (program)

Using a couple of very short functions written in JavaScript it is possible to move objects around the screen, interactively.

Below is an example given in 2008 by Ian Hickson, the editor of the HTML specification:

The plan is to show that images can be moved around the screen. Here we have two images, a moose and a cow.

```
<head>
<style>
/* We make the images a bit smaller */
    img { height: 4em; }
/* Style the <div>s so that they look like drop targets */
    div { margin: 1em 2em; border: solid black; text-align: center;
        height: 9em; width: 12em; float: left; }
/* Put the images on their own line */
    p { clear: both; margin: 1em 3em; }
</style>
</head>

<body>
<h1>Drag And Drop demo</h1>
<!--
We need to create somewhere to which we can drag these images.
One box for Friends.
The functions below are linked to the <div>s by adding 'ondrop...'.
We also need to add 'ondragenter' and 'ondragover' to permit the
    image to be copied.
-->
    <div ondrop="drop(this, event)" ondragenter="return false"
                        ondragover="return false">
    <p>Friends</p>
    </div>
<!--
and one box for Rivals
-->
    <div ondrop="drop(this, event)" ondragenter="return false"
                        ondragover="return false">
    <p>Rivals</p>
    </div>
<!--
The images - a moose and a cow.
```

It is important to always put the **alt** *attributes*

-->

    <p>

<!--

The functions below are called from each image by adding 'ondragstart'

-->

    <img src="sp_moose.gif" id=sp_moose alt="moose"
        ondragstart="drag(this, event)">
    <img src="cow8.gif" id=cow8 alt="cow" ondragstart="drag(this, event)">
    <p>

<!--

using the drag and drop API (application program interface) of HTML.
We need a function which uses the element which is being dragged,
    the target and the event, e.
We say that we are dragging some Text which, in fact, is the image.

-->

    <script>
    function drag(target, e) {
      e.dataTransfer.setData('Text', target.id);
    }
    </script>

<!--

We also need a function to drop the image into the **<div>** *which is the target.*
preventDefault is to prevent the default behaviour.

-->

    <script>
    function drop(target, e) {
    var id = e.dataTransfer.getData('Text');
    target.appendChild(document.getElementById
      (e.dataTransfer.getData("Text")));
    e.preventDefault();
    }
    </script>

List of Attributes available for each element

- List of attributes used by each element (see page 125)
- Description of the global attributes (see page 141)
- Description of the non-global attributes (see page 146)

Alphabetical:

Attributes for the `<a>` element:
global attributes

the `href` attribute - see page 154

the `target` attribute - see page 170

the `ping` attribute - see page 161

the `rel` attribute - see page 162

the `download` attribute - see page 151

the `hreflang` attribute - see page 155

the `type` attribute - see page 171

Attributes for the `<abbr>` element:
global attributes

including the `title` attribute which must and must only provide an expansion of the abbreviation - see page 142

Attributes for the `<address>` element:
global attributes only

Attributes for the `<area>` element:
global attributes

the `alt` attribute - see page 146

the `coords` attribute - see page 149

the `shape` attribute - see page 168

the `href` attribute - see page 154

the `target` attribute - see page 170

the `ping` attribute - see page 161

the `rel` attribute - see page 162

the `download` attribute - see page 151

the `hreflang` attribute - see page 155

the `type` attribute - see page 171

Attributes for the `<article>` element:
global attributes

Attributes for the `<aside>` element:
global attributes only

Attributes for the `<audio>` element:
global attributes

the `src` attribute - see page 169

the `autoplay` attribute - see page 147

the `loop` attribute - see page 156

the `controls` attribute - see page 149

the `crossorigin` attribute - see page 150

the `preload` attribute - see page 162

the `mediagroup` attribute - see page 157

the `muted` attribute - see page 159

Attributes for the `<b>` element:
global attributes only

Attributes for the `<base>` element:
global attributes

the `href` attribute - see page 154

the `target` attribute - see page 170

Attributes for the `<bdi>` element:
global attributes

Attributes for the `<bdo>` element:
global attributes

and the `dir` attribute set either to "ltr" or "rtl" - see page 141

Attributes for the `<blockquote>` element:
global attributes

the `cite` attribute - see page 148

Attributes for the `<body>` element (see page 144)
Attributes for the `<br>` element:
global attributes only

Attributes for the `<button>` element:
global attributes

the `autofocus` attribute - see page 147

the `disabled` attribute - see page 151

the `form` attribute - see page 151

the `formaction` attribute - see page 151

the `formenctype` attribute - see page 151

the `formmethod` attribute - see page 152

the `formnovalidate` attribute - see page 152

the `formtarget` attribute - see page 153

the `menu` attribute - see page 157

the `name` attribute - see page 159

the `type` attribute - see page 171

the `value` attribute - see page 173

Attributes for the `<canvas>` element:
global attributes

the `width` attribute - see page 173

the `height` attribute - see page 154

Attributes for the `<caption>` element:
global attributes only

Attributes for the `<cite>` element:
global attributes only

Attributes for the `<code>` element:
    global attributes only

Attributes for the `<col>` element:
    global attributes

    the `span` attribute - see page 169

Attributes for the `<colgroup>` element:
    global attributes

    the `span` attribute - see page 169

Attributes for the `<datalist>` element:
    global attributes only

Attributes for the `<dd>` element:
    global attributes only

Attributes for the `<del>` element:
    global attributes

    the `cite` attribute - see page 148

    the `datetime` attribute - see page 150

Attributes for the `<details>` element:
    global attributes

    the `open` attribute - see page 160

Attributes for the `<dfn>` element:
    global attributes

    and the `title` attribute provided that it only contains the definition of the term being defined - see page 142

Attributes for the `<dialog>` element:
    global attributes

    the `open` attribute - see page 160

Attributes for the `<div>` element:
    global attributes only

Attributes for the `<dl>` element:
    global attributes only

Attributes for the `<dt>` element:
    global attributes only

Attributes for the `<em>` element:
global attributes only

Attributes for the `<embed>` element:
global attributes

the `src` attribute - see page 169

the `type` attribute - see page 171

the `width` attribute - see page 173

the `height` attribute - see page 154

Attributes for the `<fieldset>` element:
global attributes

the `disabled` attribute - see page 151

the `form` attribute - see page 151

the `name` attribute - see page 159

Attributes for the `<figcaption>` element:
global attributes only

Attributes for the `<figure>` element:
global attributes only

Attributes for the `<footer>` element:
global attributes only

Attributes for the `<form>` element:
global attributes

the `accept-charset` attribute - see page 146

the `action` attribute - see page 146

the `autocomplete` attribute - see page 146

the `enctype` attribute - see page 151

the `method` attribute - see page 157

the `name` attribute - see page 159

the `novalidate` attribute - see page 159

the `target` attribute - see page 170

Attributes for the `<h1>` to `<h6>` elements:
global attributes only

Attributes for the `<head>` element:
global attributes only

Attributes for the `<header>` element:
global attributes only

Attributes for the `<hgroup>` element:
global attributes only

Attributes for the `<hr>` element:
global attributes only

Attributes for the `<html>` element:
global attributes

the `manifest` command - see page 156

Attributes for the `<i>` element:
global attributes only

Attributes for the `<iframe>` element:
global attributes

the `src` attribute - see page 169

the `srcdoc` attribute - see page 169

the `name` attribute - see page 159

the `sandbox` attribute - see page 165

the `seamless` attribute - see page 167

the `allowfullscreen` attribute - see page 146

the `width` attribute - see page 173

the `height` attribute - see page 154

Attributes for the `<img>` element:
global attributes

the `alt` attribute - see page 146

the `src` attribute - see page 169

the `srcset` attribute - see page 169

the crossorigin attribute - see page 150

the usemap attribute - see page 173

the ismap attribute - see page 155

the width attribute - see page 173

the height attribute - see page 154

Attributes for the `<input>` element:
global attributes

the accept attribute - see page 146

the alt attribute - see page 146

the autocomplete attribute - see page 146

the autofocus attribute - see page 147

the checked attribute - see page 147

the dirname attribute - see page 150

the disabled attribute - see page 151

the form attribute - see page 151

the formaction attribute - see page 151

the formenctype attribute - see page 151

the formmethod attribute - see page 152

the formnovalidate attribute - see page 152

the formtarget attribute - see page 153

the height attribute - see page 154

the inputmode attribute - see page 155

the list attribute - see page 155

the max attribute - see page 157

the maxlength attribute - see page 157

the min attribute - see page 158

the `minlength` attribute - see page 158

the `multiple` attribute - see page 158

the `name` attribute - see page 159

the `pattern` attribute - see page 160

the `placeholder` attribute - see page 161

the `readonly` attribute - see page 162

the `required` attribute - see page 163

the `size` attribute - see page 168

the `src` attribute - see page 169

the `step` attribute - see page 170

the `type` attribute - see page 171

the `value` attribute - see page 173

the `width` attribute - see page 173

Attributes for the `<ins>` element:
global attributes

`cite` attribute - see page 148

`datetime` attribute - see page 150

Attributes for the `<kbd>` element:
global attributes only

Attributes for the `<keygen>` element:
global attributes

the `autofocus` attribute - see page 147

the `challenge` attribute - see page 147

the `disabled` attribute - see page 151

the `form` attribute - see page 151

the `keytype` attribute - see page 155

the `name` attribute - see page 159

Attributes for the `<label>` element:
  global attributes

  the `for` attribute - see page 151

  the `form` attribute - see page 151

Attributes for the `<legend>` element:
  global attributes only

Attributes for the `<li>` element:
  global attributes

  and the `value` attribute if within the `<ol>` element - see page 173

Attributes for the `<link>` element:
  global attributes

  the `href` attribute - see page 154

  the `crossorigin` attribute - see page 150

  the `rel` attribute - see page 162

  the `media` attribute - see page 157

  the `hreflang` attribute - see page 155

  the `type` attribute - see page 171

  the `sizes` attribute - see page 168

Attributes for the `<main>` element:
  global attributes

Attributes for the `<map>` element:
  global attributes

  the `name` attribute - see page 159

Attributes for the `<mark>` element:
  global attributes only

Attributes for the `<menu>` element:
  global attributes

  the `type` attribute - see page 171

  the `label` attribute - see page 155

Attributes for the `<menuitem>` element:
global attributes

the `type` attribute - see page 171

the `label` attribute - see page 155

the `icon` attribute - see page 155

the `disabled` attribute - see page 151

the `checked` attribute - see page 147

the `radiogroup` attribute - see page 162

the `default` attribute - see page 150

the `command` attribute - see page 149

Attributes for the `<meta>` element:
global attributes

the `name` attribute - see page 159

the `http-equiv` attribute - see page 155

the `content` attribute - see page 149

the `charset` attribute - see page 147

Attributes for the `<meter>` element:
global attributes

the `value` attribute - see page 173

the `min` attribute - see page 158

the `low` attribute - see page 156

the `high` attribute - see page 154

the `max` attribute - see page 157

the `optimum` attribute - see page 160

Attributes for the `<nav>` element:
global attributes only

Attributes for the `<noscript>` element:
global attributes only

Attributes for the `<object>` element:
    global attributes

      the `data` attribute - see page 150

      the `type` attribute - see page 171

      the `typemustmatch` attribute - see page 173

      the `name` attribute - see page 159

      the `usemap` attribute - see page 173

      the `form` attribute - see page 151

      the `width` attribute - see page 173

      the `height` attribute - see page 154

Attributes for the `<ol>` element:
    global attributes

      the `reversed` attribute - see page 163

      the `start` attribute - see page 169

      the `type` attribute - see page 171

Attributes for the `<optgroup>` element:
    global attributes

      the `disabled` attribute - see page 151

      the `label` attribute - see page 155

Attributes for the `<option>` element:
    global attributes

      the `disabled` attribute - see page 151

      the `label` attribute - see page 155

      the `selected` attribute - see page 167

      the `value` attribute - see page 173

Attributes for the `<output>` element:
    global attributes

      the `for` attribute - see page 151

the `form` attribute - see page 151

the `name` attribute - see page 159

Attributes for the `<p>` element:
global attributes only

Attributes for the `<param>` element:
global attributes

`name` attribute - see page 159

`value` attribute - see page 173

Attributes for the `<pre>` element:
global attributes only

Attributes for the `<progress>` element:
global attributes

the `value` attribute - see page 173

the `max` attribute - see page 157

Attributes for the `<q>` element:
global attributes

the `cite` attribute - see page 148

Attributes for the `<rp>` element:
global attributes only

Attributes for the `<rt>` element:
global attributes only

Attributes for the `<ruby>` element:
global attributes only

Attributes for the `<s>` element:
global attributes only

Attributes for the `<samp>` element:
global attributes only

Attributes for the `<script>` element:
global attributes

`src` attribute - see page 169

`type` attribute - see page 171

charset attribute - see page 147

async attribute - see page 146

defer attribute - see page 150

crossorigin attribute - see page 150

Attribute for the `<section>` element:
global attributes

there is only one other attribute for this element, the cite attribute - see page 148

Attributes for the `<select>` element:
global attributes

the autocomplete attribute - see page 146

the autofocus attribute - see page 147

the disabled attribute - see page 151

the form attribute - see page 151

the multiple attribute - see page 158

the name attribute - see page 159

the required attribute - see page 163

the size attribute - see page 168

Attributes for the `<small>` element:
global attributes only

Attributes for the `<source>` element:
global attributes

the src attribute - see page 169

the type attribute - see page 171

Attributes for the `<span>` element:
global attributes only

Attributes for the `<strong>` element:
global attributes only

Attributes for the `<style>` element:
global attributes

the `media` attribute - see page 157

the `type` attribute - see page 171

the `scoped` attribute - see page 167

Attributes for the `<sub>` element:
global attributes only

Attributes for the `<summary>` element:
global attributes only

Attributes for the `<sup>` element:
global attributes only

Attributes for the `<table>` element:
global attributes

the `sortable` attribute - see page 169

Attributes for the `<tbody>` element:
global attributes only

Attributes for the `<td>` element:
global attributes

the `colspan` attribute - see page 149

the `rowspan` attribute - see page 164

the `headers` attribute - see page 153

Attributes for the `<textarea>` element:
global attributes

the `autofocus` attribute - see page 147

the `cols` attribute - see page 148

the `disabled` attribute - see page 151

the `form` attribute - see page 151

the `maxlength` attribute - see page 157

the `name` attribute - see page 159

the `placeholder` attribute - see page 161

the `readonly` attribute - see page 162

the `required` attribute - see page 163

the `rows` attribute - see page 164

the `wrap` attribute - see page 174

Attributes for the `<tfoot>` element:
global attributes only

Attributes for the `<th>` element:
global attributes

the `colspan` attribute - see page 149

the `rowspan` attribute - see page 164

the `headers` attribute - see page 153

the `scope` attribute - see page 165

the `sorted` attribute - see page 169

the `abbr` attribute - see page 146

Attributes for the `<thead>` element:
global attributes only

Attributes for the `<tr>` element:
global attributes only

Attributes for the `<track>` element:
global attributes

the `default` attribute - see page 150

the `kind` attribute - see page 155

the `label` attribute - see page 155

the `src` attribute - see page 169

the `srclang` attribute - see page 169

Attributes for the `<time>` element:
global attributes

the datetime attribute - see page 150

Attributes for the `<ul>` element:
global attributes only

Attributes for the `<var>` element:
global attributes only

Attributes for the `<video>` element:
global attributes

the src attribute - see page 169

the crossorigin attribute - see page 150

the preload attribute - see page 162

the mediagroup attribute - see page 157

the muted attribute - see page 159

the poster attribute - see page 162

the autoplay attribute - see page 147

the loop attribute - see page 156

the controls attribute - see page 149

the width attribute - see page 173

the height attribute - see page 154

Attributes for the `<wbr>` element:
global attributes only

Some attributes are boolean attributes. That means that the presence of the attribute indicates that it is true, its absence means it is false.

Global attributes

The following attributes are common to and may be specified on all HTML elements:

- accesskey which specifies a keyboard shortcut to access an element
- class is used to identify and apply styles named in a CSS file, for example:

  .highlight { background: yellow; }

  could be used to emphasize the Shakespeare/Bacon controversy in the following example:

  ... and henceforth he shines forth in English verse and drama under one only name as Shakespeare*, the greatest genius of all times and nations.*

  The markup is:

  ... and henceforth he shines forth in English verse and drama <span class="highlight">under one only name as Shakespeare</span>, the greatest genius of all times and nations.
- contenteditable specifies whether or not a user is permitted to edit the content
- contextmenu represents a shortcut menu typically being the default action of a mouseup or keyup event.
- dir represents the direction (left to right or right to left) of text. In particular it can be used for text, like Hebrew, which is written right to left.
- draggable enables the user to drag (and drop) text or pictures (for example). <a> elements with an href attribute and <img> elements have their draggable attribute set to true by default.

  See also an example of Drag and Drop using JavaScript on page 123.
- hidden indicates that the element is not yet, or is no longer, relevant. For example it could be used to hide something until the user logs in. In a script it could be used like this:

  document.getElementById('login').hidden = true;
  document.getElementById('member').hidden = false;

- id represents its element's unique identifier. It may not contain any spaces.

  Example:

  <h2 id="introduction">Introduction</h2>
  <p>This work attempts to explain how to create a web page using the latest version of HTML</p>

and later in the same document

```
<h2 id="index">Index</h2>
<ul>
<li>...</li>
<li><a href="#introduction">Introduction</a></li>
</ul>
```

Note that the old `name` tag is no longer supported in HTML.

- `item` identifies blocks to be marked as structure data as a group of name-value pairs
- `itemprop` attribute is used when encoding microdata which consists of groups of name-value pairs known as items.
- `lang` attribute specifies the primary language for the element's content. Example:

   The memoirs of Marguerite preceded what is known in French history as *La Guerre amoureuse*, and form the foundation round which the play of *Love's Labour's Lost* is built up.

   Here is the markup:

   The memoirs of Marguerite preceded what is known in French history as <cite lang=fr>La Guerre amoureuse</cite>, and form the foundation round which the play of <cite>Love's Labour's Lost</cite> is built up.

   Note that the citation for *Love's Labour's Lost* does not use the `lang` attribute since the default language is English.
- `spellcheck` attribute is used for spelling and grammar checking and is either true or false.
- `style` attribute can be used to incorporate CSS styles within the html document. Personally I would discourage them in favour of incorporating all styles within a CSS file.

   Be aware that if the `<style>` were to be removed that the document must remain comprehensible without this style. That is the `<style>` is only presentational and should not affect the meaning.
- `subject` attribute is used when encoding microdata which consists of groups of name-value pairs known as items.
- `tabindex`. This is an attribute which indicates which element has the focus (the next to be dealt with). Its name comes from the common use of the "tab" key to navigate from one place to another.
- `title` attribute enables information about the element to be passed to the user. It could be used as a tooltip or a description of an image.

   For example: <img src="picture.jpg", alt="description of the picture if it is not visible" title="My dog, Alfred">

   It has special meaning for the `<link>`, `<style>`, `<dfn>` and `<abbr>` elements.

In addition the following attributes may be specified on any HTML element:

- `onabort`
- `oncanplay`
- `oncanplaythrough`

- onchange
- onclick
- oncontextmenu
- ondblclick
- ondrag
- ondragend
- ondragenter
- ondragleave
- ondragover
- ondragstart
- ondrop
- ondurationchange
- onemptied
- onended
- onformchange
- onforminput
- oninput
- oninvalid
- onkeydown
- onkeypress
- onkeyup
- onloadeddata
- onloadedmetadata
- onloadstart
- onmousedown
- onmousemove
- onmouseout
- onmouseover
- onmouseup
- onmousewheel
- onpagehide
- onpageshow
- onpause
- onplay
- onplaying
- onprogress
- onratechange
- onreadystatechange
- onscroll
- onseeked
- onseeking
- onselect
- onshow
- onstalled
- onsubmit

- `onsuspend`
- `ontimeupdate`
- `onvolumechange`
- `onwaiting`

...and the following ("on") event attributes may be used with the `<body>` element:

- `onafterprint`
- `onbeforeprint`
- `onbeforeunload`
- `onhashchange`
- `onmessage`
- `onoffline`
- `ononline`
- `onpagehide`
- `onpageshow`
- `onpopstate`
- `onstorage`
- `onunload`

However there are four special attributes, `onblur`, `onerror`, `onfocus` and `onload`, which may be used with the `<body>` element but do not "bubble" (that is propogate back to the `<body>` element when used on other elements):

- `onfocus` "fires" (that is attempts to start an event) when an element receives focus either via the pointing device (mouse, trackball, joystick, touchpad, light pen etc) or by tab navigation
- `onblur` "fires" when an element loses focus either via the pointing device or by tab navigation.
- `onload` "fires" when the "user agent" (the browser) finishes loading all content within a document, which includes the window, frames, objects and images. For elements, it fires when the target element and all its content has finished loading.
- `onerror` "fires" when an object, image or frame cannot be loaded properly

Not all events bubble. You can set whether an even bubbles or not when you create it.

These attributes when used on any element may result in the action specified by that attribute for the `<body>` element.

However, as stated in the introduction, I do not intend to explain here, how each of these events can be used. A good book on JavaScript is recommended.

An example of the use of one of these attributes is when wishing to put the focus (the curser) in a certain field when showing a form:

```
<body onload="focusonfield()">
```

Another use is the `<form>` itself:

```
<form onsubmit="return required()">
```

Other attributes (non-global)

- `abbr` is only used as an attribute for the `<th>` element. It is an alternative label to be used for the header cell when referencing the cell in other contexts.
- `accept` is used to show what type of files may be accepted, for example *audio*, *video*, *image*, *text* and they must be separated by commas.
  Example:

  [   ] [Browse...]

  and the markup:
  `<input type="file" name="myvideo" accept="video/quicktime,audio/mpeg">`
- `accept-charset` is used to show which character sets the server can use, for example
    - ISO-8859-1 for the Latin alphabet
    - UTF-8 for Unicode
    - windows-1252 to accept windows only
    - US-ASCII to accept ascii characters

  It must be an ordered set of unique space separated tokens.
  Example:
  `<form accept-charset="UTF-8">`
- `action` must take the user to a valid URL, that is to a page or program which activates the query of the form.
  Example:
  `<form action="user_response.p1">`
- `allowfullscreen`, if present, allows the contents of the `<iframe>>` to be shown full screen.
- `alt`
    - for images - must contain text which describes what one would see if the image was not there for any reason
    - for buttons which only contain an image - must contain text which conveys the purpose of the button
    - for the `<area>` element it is there to specify the text of the hyperlink, if any. In this case if there is no hyperlink then the `alt` attribute must be omitted
    - for the `<input>` element it must provide text for users who cannot see the image. It must always be present and non blank if there is an image

  If the absence of the image makes absolutely no difference then it is permissable to write alt="".
- `async` allows the script, if available, to be executed.
- `autocomplete` should be set to "off" for sensitive data, for example a pin number and should be set to "on" for values that are not sensitive and you would like the browser to remember. The default state is the absence

of this attribute, which could depend on the browser's interpretation. Example:

Name: [   ]

and the markup:
Name: <input type="text" name="surname" size=30 autocomplete=on>

- autofocus enables the user to enter data into the selected field immediately that the form appears on the page. Obviously no more than one element in the document may have the autofocus attribute.

Surname [   ] *First name* [   ]

the markup is:

> *<p>Surname <input type="text" name="surname" value=""*
> *autofocus>*
> *First name <input type="text" name="firstname" value=""></p>*

and if the user starts typing, the data will automatically start in the first box, surname.

- autoplay. When this attribute is present, playback will start automatically, however this is not to be encouraged as it is considered preferable to let the user decide when to start playback.
- challenge. The <keygen> element (only) permits the use of this attribute.
- charset represents the character encoding, example: "utf-8"
- checked.

This attribute will preselect a value if the type attribute is in the Checkbox state or the Radio state.

Please reserve seats:

- ● Most expensive
- ○ Average
- ○ Very cheap

and the markup:

> *<p>Please reserve seats:</p>*
> *<ul>*
> *<li><input type="radio" name="seats" value="expensive"*
> *checked="checked">*
> *Most expensive</li>*
> *<li><input type="radio" name="seats" value="medium">*
> *Average</li>*
> *<li><input type="radio" name="seats" value="cheap">*

Very cheap</li>
</ul>

- `<cite>` The difference between the `<cite>` element and the `cite` attribute is that the latter must give a valid URL (see page 6) to the original source whilst the former represents the title of a work. For example:

Dennis Whitmore wrote an article called *Game Theory* in which he writes:

Game theory is concerned with decision making and strategy and is used where there is conflict against an *opponent* such as rival organizations. It is a sort of "cat-and-mouse" strategy, trying to out-guess and predict outcomes and the opposition's strategies.

the markup is:

<p>Dennis Whitmore wrote an article called <cite>Game Theory</cite> in which he writes:</p>
<blockquote cite="httl://www.managers-net.org/gametheory.html">
Game theory is concerned with decision making and strategy and is used where there is conflict against
an opponent such as rival organizations.
It is a sort of "cat-and-mouse" strategy, trying to out-guess and predict outcomes and the opposition's strategies.
</blockquote>

Browsers should permit users to follow these citation links.
The `<del>` and `<ins>` elements should use the `cite` attribute to show the URL of the changes whilst the `<section>` element would use it if content is taken from another page.
If the source is fictional then this attribute cannot be used.
- `cols` specifies the maximum number of characters per line before wrapping takes place.

- colspan enables cells to span across more than one column and its counterpart, the rowspan attribute may span down more than one row. Example:

Education	
Company run Schools	27
Child Care Centres	83

Note that here there are three rows, so three pairs of <tr>...</tr> the markup is:

```
<table>
<tr>
<th colspan=2>Education</th>
</tr>
<tr>
<td>Company run Schools</td>
<td>27</td>
</tr>
<tr>
<td>Child Care Centres</td>
<td>83</td>
</tr>
</table>
```

For rowspan - see page 164
- command. This is the command definition used with <menuitem>.
- content. This is the text for the <meta> element in the header (see page 9) of the document.
- controls. Use this attribute if you wish to let the browser provide the audio and video controls for you. Its absence means that you will have to write a script yourself to provide the controls, play, pause, volume etc. Thus <audio src="noise.wav" controls><audio>, the browser does the work for you, <audio src="noise.wav" ><audio>, you must provide a script.
- coords. This attribute must be specifed for the following shapes: **circle**, **rectangle** and **polygon** and must contain a set of integers (whole numbers).
  For a circle it is necessary to give (measurements in pixels),
  1. the distance from the left edge of the image to the centre of the circle
  2. the distance from the top of the image to the centre of the circle
  3. the radius of the circle
  For a rectangle it is necessary to give exactly four integers,
  1. the distance from the left edge of the image to the left edge of the rectangle
  2. the distance from the top of the image to the top of the rectangle

3. the distance from the left edge of the image to the right edge of the rectangle
4. the distance from the top of the image to the bottom of the rectangle

For a polygon there must be at least three pairs of coordinates, each pair representing one point of the shape:

1. the *x* coordinate of the point
2. the *y* coordinate of the point

For an example of the coordinates of a polygon - see page 92

Note that each coordinate must be separated by a 'comma' character, *with no other characters (e.g. no space characters)* between them.

The `coords` attribute must *not* be specified for the default state, that is the whole image.

- `crossorigin`. The main security and privacy implications of the `<video>` and `<audio>` elements come from the ability to embed media cross-origin. It could be relatively easy for a hostile programmer to insert code into a source from a different domain which is called by your program. The `crossorigin>` attribute allows authors to control how checks are made to avoid this.

- `data`, if present, must specify the address (URL) of the resource. If the `data` attribute is not present then the `type` attribute must be present. Example:

  <figure>
  <object data="clock.html"></object>
  <legend>Time piece</legend>
  </figure>

- `datetime`, if present, must contain a valid date or time or both or be empty. For example, a valid datetime is
  YYYY-MM-DDThh:mm:ssTZD **where:**
    - YYYY is the year (ex. 2010)
    - MM is the month in digits (ex. 06 for June)
    - DD is the day of the month (ex. 30)
    - T is required to separate the date from the time
    - hh is for the hour (ex. 13 for 1pm)
    - mm is for the minutes (ex. 55)
    - ss is for the seconds (ex. 55)
    - TZD (Time Zone Designator) denotes the time zone, "Z" (ZULU) is the zero meridian or GMT, the zones to the east of London around the world are lettered "A" to "M", ("J" is not used), whilst the zones to the west of London are lettered "N" to "Y"

- `default`. A boolean attribute, this marks the command in the `<menuitem>` element or the track in the `<track>` element as being the default.

- `defer`. A boolean attribute to defer the execution of the script.

- `dirname`. The name of the form field with the element `<textarea>`.

- disabled. A form or other controls are disabled, a command is not available, an option or a group of options is disabled, if its disabled attribute is set, that is, the disabled attribute is present.
- download>. Whether to download the resource instead of navigating to it, and add its filename if present.
- enctype is an attribute that you will probably not need to use. It determines how form data is encoded and has three possible values:
  - application/x-www-form-urlencoded *(the default value)*
  - multipart/form-data *(used for file uploads)*
  - text/plain

In this example, the enctype attribute is used to send form data unencoded:

```
<form action="address.php" method="get" enctype="text/plain">
...
</form>
```

- for. It is important to associate <label> elements with form controls. For the <output> element it allows an explicit relationship to be made between the result of a calculation and the elements that represent the values that went into or otherwise influenced the calculation. In both cases it takes the value of an id of an element in the same document. Example:

```
<form>
<label for="male">Male</label>
<input type="radio" name="sex" id="male">
<label for="female">Female</label>
<input type="radio" name="sex" id="female">
</form>
```

which should look like this:

Male ◯ Female ◯

- form Its value must be the id of a <form> element in the same document. It would be used to associate <form> elements with form controls. It is not frequently used.
- formaction, like the action attribute must have a valid URL and will send the user's input to a new page called by that URL.
- formenctype, like enctype has three possible values:
  - application/x-www-form-urlencoded *(the default value)*
  - multipart/form-data *(used for file uploads)*
  - text/plain

In this example, the formenctype attribute is used to send form data unencoded:

```
<form action="address.php" method="get" formenctype="text/plain">
...
</form>
```

If the element is a submit `<button>` then it uses the `formenctype` attribute and the element's `enctype` is that attribute's state.

- `formmethod` and the `method` attributes have the following keywords:
  - GET
  - POST
  - PUT
  - DELETE

The GET method is used for retrieving data, for example, a query where the data does not change, whereas POST is used for storing or updating data. If for example you used the POST method and you enter sensitive data (a credit card number), press submit, leave the room and somebody else comes and presses the back button, the browser *might* give a warning and not permit the return to the screen with the sensitive data. The PUT method is the best way to request the uploading of files. It involves less handling by the server-side handler.

The DELETE method should ignore the form data and access and delete the file specified by `action`.

If the element is a submit `<button>` then it uses the `formmethod` attribute otherwise it uses the `method` attribute.

- `formnovalidate` (and `novalidate`), if present, indicate that the form is not to be validated during submission.

This attribute is useful to include "save" buttons on forms that have validation constraints, to allow users to save their progress even though they haven't fully entered the data in the form. The following example shows a simple form that has two required fields. There are three buttons: one to submit the form, which requires both fields to be filled in; one to save the form so that the user can come back and fill it in later; and one to cancel the form altogether.

Example of formnovalidate

Name: [   ]

Essay: [   ]

Submit essay | Save essay | Cancel

This attribute (`formnovalidate`) is an attribute of the `<input>` element.

Below is the markup:

```
<form action="editor.cgi" method="post">
<fieldset>
```

```
<legend>Example of formnovalidate</legend>
<p><label>Name: <input type="text"
        required name=fn></label></p>
<p><label>Essay: <textarea name=essay rows="2" cols="25">
        </textarea></label></p>
<p><input type=submit name=submit value="Submit essay">
   <input type=submit formnovalidate name=save
        value="Save essay">
   <input type=submit formnovalidate name=cancel
        value="Cancel"></p>
</fieldset>
</form>
```

- `formtarget` is used with the `<button>` and `<input>` elements, otherwise it is the same as the `target` attribute (see page 170)
- `headers`. This attribute allows text-only browsers (screen readers) to render the header information for a given cell. It makes no difference in ordinary browsers.

Half Marathon Results

Position	Name	Time	PB
28th	Chris Bryant	1:28:02	PB
29th	Peter Smith	1:28:04	PB

... and the markup:

```
<table>
<caption>Half Marathon Results</caption>
<thead>
 <tr>
 <th id="position">Position</th>
 <th id="name">Name</th>
 <th id="time">Time</th>
 <th id="PB">PB</th>
 </tr>
</thead>
<tbody>
 <tr>
 <td headers="position">28th</td>
 <td headers="name">Chris Bryant</td>
 <td headers="time">1:28:02</td>
 <td headers="PB">PB</td>
 </tr>
 <tr>
 <td headers="position">29th</td>
 <td headers="name">Peter Smith</td>
 <td headers="time">1:28:04</td>
 <td headers="PB">PB</td>
 </tr>
```

</tbody>
</table>

- `height` and `width` attributes may be specified to give the dimensions of the picture or image which you wish to display. They are not intended to stretch the image, indeed, if you wish to display an image using the `<img>` element it is better to resize the picture using a program such as 'The Gimp' and then to omit these attributes altogether.
  An example of the markup is:

  <embed src="../actionwork/bullying.avi" height=150 width=100>

- `high` is one of six attributes used by the `<meter>` element. The other attributes are `low`, `value`, `min`, `max` and `optimum`.
  - The `min` attribute specifies the lower bound of the range,
  - the `max` attribute specifies the upper bound of the range,
  - the `value` attribute specifies the "measured" value which the gauge should indicate,
  - the `low` attribute specifies what is considered a "low" value whilst
  - the `high` attribute specifies what is considered to be the "high" value.
  - The `optimum` attribute shows the position of the gauge which is considered to be the "optimum".

  Not all the attributes need to be specified.
  These examples are equivalent:

  <meter>35%</meter>
  <meter low="10" high="48" value="35"></meter>

- `href` attribute must have a valid URL which will be a link to another resource (destination somewhere else in the same document, another webpage, pdf file etc).
  Examples:

  In the **introduction** we mentioned that web pages must always be kept up-to-date.

  One of my sons and his wife have built a magnificent **hotel** in Greece.

  The markup is:

  <p>In the <a href="#introduction">introduction</a>
  we mentioned that web pages must always be kept up-to-date.</p>
  <p>One of my sons and his wife have built a magnificent

<a href="http://www.traveldevel.org/hotel/">hotel</a>
in Greece.</p>

There is another example for the use of the href attribute used with the
<area> element shown in the description of the <map> element (see
page 92).

- hreflang. The use of this attribute gives the language of the linked
resource. It is purely advisory. It enables the browser to avoid presenting
garbage to the user or may be able to explain the reason.
Example:

Domnista is a small village in the Greek mountains

and the markup:

<p><a href="http://www.domnista.gr" hreflang="gr">
Domnista</a> is a small village in the Greek mountains</p>

- http-equiv Pragma directive. Useful if the content of the page
changes regularly.
- icon. This enables a picture, usually very small, to represent the
command in the element <menuitem>> Example:

<menuitem onclick="alert('gearbox')" icon="gear.ico"
label="Run through gears">

- inputmode. An indication of the type of input to expect, for example:
verbatim, latin-text, numeric, telephone, email ...
- ismap indicates that the <img> element provides access to a server-
side image map. It is only used with the <img> element which must be
preceded by the <a> element and the href attribute. ismap is a
boolean attribute, that is its use is ismap="ismap" or ismap="".

<a href="Thomas_History.html"><img src="thomas.jpg"
alt="Thomas has red hair and a long nose"
ismap="ismap"></a>

- keytype, as its name suggests, gives the type of key being used for the
element <keygen>. The only value suggested at the time of writing is
keytype="rsa".
- kind. The type of text track.
- label. For the <menu> element it is used by the browser to display
nested menus and gives a label to the menu. In the case of the element
<optgroup> it must be specified, to give a name to each group as seen
by the user. For other elements it is a user-visible label.
- list is used to identify options from a, or several, predefined input lists
made available to the user. It must have the same name as the id of a

`<datalist>` in the same document. An example is given with the description of the `<datalist>` element (see page 115).

- `loop`. This attribute enables a media resource to keep repeating itself automatically.
  Example:

  <audio src="rain.avi" loop>It just won't stop raining</audio>

- `low` is one of six attributes used by the `<meter>` element. The other attributes are `high`, `value`, `min`, `max` and `optimum`.
  - The `min` attribute specifies the lower bound of the range,
  - the `max` attribute specifies the upper bound of the range,
  - the `value` attribute specifies the "measured" value which the gauge should indicate,
  - the `low` attribute specifies what is considered a "low" value whilst
  - the `high` attribute specifies what is considered to be the "high" value.
  - The `optimum` attribute shows the position of the gauge which is considered to be the "optimum".

  Not all the attributes need to be specified.
  These examples are equivalent:

  <meter>35%</meter>
  <meter low="10" high="48" value="35"></meter>

- `manifest`. This is used to run web applications off-line. Basically it saves all the files needed for an application in a cache in your computer so that you can work off-line. For example let's consider a program which shows you the route between San Francisco and Yosemite, a two day drive. When you get tired you may decide to find an hotel. The program is called "route.html". It uses a CSS file called "preference.css" and a JavaScript script called "route.js". To create a manifest of these three files we could write the program like this:

  <!DOCTYPE HTML>
  <html>
  <head>
  <title>Route</title>
  <script src="route.js"></script>
  <link rel="stylesheet" href="preferred.css">
  </head>
  <body>
  <p> ... </p>
  </body>
  </html>

As night draws in you decide to look for an hotel. The program is still available on your laptop although there is no link to the internet.

- `max` is one of six attributes used by the `<meter>` element. The other attributes are `low`, `high`, `value`, `min` and `optimum`.
  - The `min` attribute specifies the lower bound of the range,
  - the `max` attribute specifies the upper bound of the range,
  - the `value` attribute specifies the "measured" value which the gauge should indicate,
  - the `low` attribute specifies what is considered a "low" value whilst
  - the `high` attribute specifies what is considered to be the "high" value.
  - The `optimum` attribute shows the position of the gauge which is considered to be the "optimum".

Not all the attributes need to be specified.

These examples are equivalent:

<meter>75%</meter>
<meter min="0" max="100" value="75"></meter>

- `maxlength`. If the `<input>` element has a maximum allowed length, then the value of the `value` attribute must be no more than the `maxlength`. Likewise if the `<textarea>` element has a maximum allowed length, then the number of characters entered into this area must not exceed (or will be shortened to) this value.
- `media` is purely advisory.

  It can be omitted, the default indicating that the resource applies to all media. If included it describes for which media the document was designed. Examples are media="screen" and media="print". Other possible values include braille, handheld, projection, tty, tv, embossed and speech.

  When used with the `<picture>` element it can also have values such as min-with, max-height, device-width, device-height, orientation, aspect-ration, color, monochrome, resolution and grid.

- `mediagroup`. Groups media elements (`<audio>` and `<video>`) together.
- `menu`. Specifies the element's designated popup menu.
- `method` and the `formmethod` attributes have the following keywords:
  - `GET`
  - `POST`
  - `PUT`
  - `DELETE`

The GET method is used for retrieving data, for example, a query where the data does not change, whereas POST is used for storing or updating data. If for example you used the `POST` method and you enter sensitive data (a credit card number), press submit, leave the room and somebody else comes and presses the back button, the browser *might* give a warning and not permit the return to the screen with the sensitive data. The `PUT` method is the best way to request the uploading of files. It involves less handling by the server-side handler.

The `DELETE` method should ignore the form data and access and delete the file specified by `action`.

Example:

```
<form
    name="userform"
    onSubmit="return required()"
    method="POST"
    action="userresponse.p1">
```

where "userform" is the name of the form used when defining the fields, e.g. username = document.userform.surname.value;

"return required()" refers to the function called "required()" and is the initial action to be taken when the form is submitted,

"method" is as described above, and

"action" refers to the name of the program or document which will carry out the follow-up.

- `min` is one of six attributes used by the `<meter>` element. The other attributes are `low`, `high`, `value`, `max` and `optimum`.
  - The `min` attribute specifies the lower bound of the range,
  - the `max` attribute specifies the upper bound of the range,
  - the `value` attribute specifies the "measured" value which the gauge should indicate,
  - the `low` attribute specifies what is considered a "low" value whilst
  - the `high` attribute specifies what is considered to be the "high" value.
  - The `optimum` attribute shows the position of the gauge which is considered to be the "optimum".

Not all the attributes need to be specified.

These examples are equivalent:

```
<meter>75%</meter>
<meter min="0" max="100" value="75"></meter>
```

- `minlength`. The minimum length of the value.
- `multiple`. The `multiple` attribute indicates whether the user is allowed to specify more than one value.

Members of the Carrot family

Cultivated	**Choose Carrots**	**Reset**
Chervil		
Celery		
Celeriac		
Arracacha		
Fennel		
Parsnip		
Parsley		

To select more than one type of carrot press Control + Left mouse button.
Here is the markup:

```
<fieldset>
  <legend>Members of the Carrot family</legend>
  <form action="http://carrots_anywhere.com/test" method="post">
    <select multiple size="4" name="carrot_type-select">
      <option selected value="Cultivated">Cultivated</option>
      <option selected value="Chervil">Chervil</option>
      <option>Celery</option>
      <option>Celeriac</option>
      <option>Arracacha</option>
      <option>Fennel</option>
      <option>Parsnip</option>
      <option>Parsley</option>
    </select>
    <button type="submit" name="send">Choose Carrots</button>
    <button type="reset">Reset</button>
  </form>
</fieldset>
```

In this example the `size` attribute has been set to 4. This gives the number of options that the user will see, although there may be a lot more available.
Here I have preselected 2 types of carrot, thus that will be the default choice. The user can change this.

- `muted`. Whether or not to mute the media resource by default.
- `name`, when used with the `<iframe>`, `<object>` and `<param>` elements it names the element. It *must* be present with the `<param>` element to give the name of the parameter.
When used with the `<map>` element it must be present to give a name to the map so that it can be referenced.
For the `<form>` element it represents the form's name.
For the other elements (`<fieldset>`, `<input>`, `<object>`, `<select>`, `<textarea>`, `<keygen>` and `<output>`) where it may be used, it gives the name of the form control.
- `novalidate` (and `formnovalidate` (see page 152)), if present, indicate that the form is not to be validated during submission.

Note that the attribute `novalidate` is to be used with the element `<form>` and the attribute `formnovalidate` is to be used with the element `<input>`.

Example of the `novalidate` attribute:

e-mail: [_____] | **Submit**

... and the markup:

```
<form action="editor.cgi" novalidate>
  e-mail: <input type="email" name="championship">
  <input type="submit">
</form>
```

- `open`. If present this attribute indicates that the `<details>` are to be shown to the user, otherwise they are to be hidden.
- `optimum` is one of six attributes used by the `<meter>` element. If the optimum value is higher than the `high` attribute's value, then the optimum value should be as high as possible, on the other hand if it is lower than the `low` attribute's value, then the lower the better. The other attributes are `low`, `high`, `value`, `min` and `max`.
  - The `min` attribute specifies the lower bound of the range,
  - the `max` attribute specifies the upper bound of the range,
  - the `value` attribute specifies the "measured" value which the gauge should indicate,
  - the `low` attribute specifies what is considered a "low" value whilst
  - the `high` attribute specifies what is considered to be the "high" value.
  - The `optimum` attribute shows the position of the gauge which is considered to be the "optimum".

Not all the attributes need to be specified, instead the default values would be used.

```
<meter low="32" high="90" optimum="99" min="0"
       max="100" value="85"></meter>
```

- `pattern`. This enables the data that is entered to be validated against a prefixed format. It is recommended that when using the `pattern` attribute on the `<input>` element that the `title` attribute be used as well so that the browser may indicate to the user the nature of any error.

Examples:

Part number: [_____]

An error on the part of the user could result in a message such as:

A part number is a digit followed by four lowercase letters.
You cannot complete this form until the field is correct.

The markup for this is:

```
<label>Part number:
  <input type="text" pattern="[0-9] [a-z] {4}" name="part_no"
    title="A part number is a digit followed by
    four lowercase letters.">
</label>
```

A few other patterns:
- ^ indicates the start of a string
- \d indicates a digit character
- $ indicates the end of a string
- \b matches any word boundary
- \B matches any non-word boundary
- \n matches a new line character
- \f matches a form feed character

and there are many more ...

- `ping` gives the URLs of the resources (list of servers) that are interested in being notified if the user breaks the hyperlink.
It allows the user to see the final target URL unobscured, it permits the browser to inform the user about out-of-band notifications and it allows the paranoid user to disable the notifications without losing the underlying link functionality.
Example:

```
<a href="#top" ping="http://blabla.com">
```

If you are thinking of using this, question well for what it could be used first.
- `placeholder` is rather like the `title` attribute, only shorter. It is intended to aid the user with the data entry.
Example:

10K race entry

Name: [   ]

Running Club: [   ]

Sex: [   ]

Age: [   ]

Here is the markup:

```
<fieldset>
 <legend>10K race entry</legend>
 <p><label>Name: <input type="text" name="fullname"
  placeholder="John Smith"
  title="Please enter your full name, both first name a space
     and then your surname"></label></p>
 <p><label>Running Club: <input type="text" name="club"
  placeholder="Leeds AC"></label></p>
 <p><label>Sex: <input type="text" name="sex"
  placeholder="M or F"></label></p>
 <p><label>Age: <input type="text" name="age"
  placeholder="36"></label></p>
</fieldset>
```

Normally you would not use the `placeholder` attribute together with the `title` attribute. It is put here to show the difference.

- `poster`. This is used so that if the video is not available, instead of showing nothing, an image which is representative of the video is presented to the user.
Example:

```
<video src="http://actionwork/silentscream.avi"
 poster="http://bullybox.co.uk/images/ss.jpg">
  The video is not available</video>
```

- `preload`. Hints as to how much buffering the media resource is likely to need. Options: "none", "metadata" and "auto".
- `radiogroup`. It defines the name of the (radio) group to which this command belongs. This should only be used if the `type` attribute (of the `<menuitem>` element which must form part of a menu) is in the radio state (`type="radio"`).
- `readonly`. The `readonly` attribute controls whether or not the user can edit the form control. Thus if it is specified on an `<input>` element, once entered it cannot be changed.
- `rel` For the `<a>` and `<area>` elements these are the permitted values for the `rel` attribute:
  - `alternate` Gives alternate representations of the current document.
  - `archives` Provides a link to a collection of records, documents, or other materials of historical interest.
  - `author` Gives a link to the current document's author.
  - `bookmark` Gives the permalink for the nearest ancestor section.
  - `external` Indicates that the referenced document is not part of the same site as the current document.
  - `feed` Gives the address of a syndication feed for the current document.

- ◦ `first` Indicates that the current document is a part of a series, and that the first document in the series is the referenced document.
- ◦ `help` Provides a link to context-sensitive help.
- ◦ `index` Gives a link to the document that provides a table of contents or index listing the current document.
- ◦ `last` Indicates that the current document is a part of a series, and that the last document in the series is the referenced document.
- ◦ `license` Indicates that the main content of the current document is covered by the copyright license described by the referenced document.
- ◦ `next` Indicates that the current document is a part of a series, and that the next document in the series is the referenced document.
- ◦ `nofollow` Indicates that the current document's original author or publisher does not endorse the referenced document.
- ◦ `noreferrer` Requires that the user agent not send an HTTP `Referer` (sic) header if the user follows the hyperlink.
- ◦ `prev` Indicates that the current document is a part of a series, and that the previous document in the series is the referenced document.
- ◦ `search` Gives a link to a resource that can be used to search through the current document and its related pages.
- ◦ `sidebar` Specifies that the referenced document, if retrieved, is intended to be shown in the browser's sidebar (if it has one).
- ◦ `tag` Gives a tag (identified by the given address) that applies to the current document.
- ◦ `up` Provides a link to a document giving the context for the current document.

Well, yes! it took me some time to understand this. Let's take an example
<a href="http://somewebpage.info/200906holiday.html" rel="bookmark">My last holiday</a>
First a "permalink" is a blogger's term for a "permanent link". That means that he may frequently write blogs and each new blog pushes the previous blog into the archives. By having a system, like using date and time or in this case Year, month, title, it will have a permanent address which won't be overwritten - ever. So the blogs are bookmarked for reference and can always be reread.

- • `required`. A long desired attribute, at last introduced in HTML. It means that an entry is required for this field in order to submit the form.

  <input type="text" name="surname" size="20" required>

- • `reversed`. Enables you to reverse the order of an ordered list:

Normal ordered list

1. Top
2. Middle
3. Bottom

Reversed ordered list

3. Top
2. Middle
1. Bottom

and the markup:

```
<h3>Normal ordered list</h3>
<ol>
  <li>Top</li>
  <li>Middle</li>
  <li>Bottom</li>
</ol>
<h3>Reversed ordered list</h3>
<ol reversed>
  <li>Top</li>
  <li>Middle</li>
  <li>Bottom</li>
</ol>
```

- `rows` specifies the number of lines to show.
- `rowspan` enables cells to span down more than one row and its counterpart, the `colspan` attribute may span across more than one column.
  Example:

Education	Company run Schools	27
	Child Care Centres	83

Note that here there are only two rows, so only two pairs of <tr>...</tr>
The markup is:

```
<table>
<tr>
 <th rowspan=2>Education</th>
 <td>Company run Schools</td>
 <td>27</td>
</tr>
<tr>
 <td>Child Care Centres</td>
 <td>83</td>
</tr>
</table>
```

For `colspan` - see page 149

- `sandbox` enables a set of extra restrictions on any content which is within the `<iframe>` element. Its possible values are:
  - allow-same-origin - allows access if from the same web site
  - allow-forms - allows forms
  - allow-scripts - allows scripts except popups

When it is set, forms and scripts are disabled, links are prevented from targeting other web sites and plugins are disabled. When fully sandoxed (*sandbox=""*), the iframe cannot open new windows. The purpose of this attribute is to allow access to other web sites without them being able to 'attack' you, that is, to make you more secure.

In this example, some completely unknown, potentially hostile, content is embedded in a web page:

```
<iframe sandbox src="getusercontent.cgi?12345"></iframe>
```

- `scope`. This has four explicit keywords:
  - row - this cell provides header information for the rest of the row
  - col - this cell provides header information for the rest of the column
  - rowgroup - this cell provides header information for the rest of the rowgroup
  - colgroup - this cell provides header information for the rest of the colgroup

The missing value, the auto state, makes the header cell apply to a set of cells selected based on context. For example the scope means that the headers refer to, or apply directly to, all the rest of the cells in the rest of the group defined by the keyword.

A	B	C	D
not here	scope=rowgroup	applies here	applies here
not here	applies here	applies here	applies here
not here	applies here	applies here	applies here

and the markup:

```
<table>
<thead>
<tr>
<th>A</th>
<th>B</th>
<th>C</th>
<th>D</th>
</tr>
</thead>
<tbody>
<tr>
```

```
<td>not here</td>
<th scope=rowgroup>scope=rowgroup</th>
<td>applies here</td>
<td>applies here</td>
</tr>
<tr>
<td>not here</td>
<td>applies here</td>
<td>applies here</td>
<td>applies here</td>
</tr>
<tr>
<td>not here</td>
<td>applies here</td>
<td>applies here</td>
<td>applies here</td>
</tr>
</tbody>
</table>
```

Here is another example which uses colgroup, col and row:

400 metre challenge						
Name	Race 1	Race 2	Race 3	Race 4	Race 5	Total
Fred Smith	1	2	1	1	3	8
John Jones	2	1	2	3	1	9
Michael Denison	3	3	3	2	2	13

'400 metre challenge', a colgroup, shows that all the columns below it
are relevant to this title. The headings in the second row are the headings
for each column, hence, scope=col, but the information in each row,
starting with a name, is relevant to that person only, hence, scope=row.

Here is the markup:

```
<table>
<thead>
 <tr>
 <th colspan="7" scope="colgroup">400 metre challenge</th>
 </tr>
</thead>
<tbody>
 <tr>
 <th scope="col">Name</th>
 <th scope="col">Race 1</th>
```

```
<th scope="col">Race 2</th>
<th scope="col">Race 3</th>
<th scope="col">Race 4</th>
<th scope="col">Race 5</th>
<th scope="col">Total</th>
</tr>
<tr>
<th scope="row">Fred Smith</th>
<td>1</td>
<td>2</td>
<td>1</td>
<td>1</td>
<td>3</td>
<th>8</th>
</tr>
<tr>
<th scope="row">John Jones</th>
<td>2</td>
<td>1</td>
<td>2</td>
<td>3</td>
<td>1</td>
<th>9</th>
</tr>
<tr>
<th scope="row">Michael Denison</th>
<td>3</td>
<td>3</td>
<td>3</td>
<td>2</td>
<td>2</td>
<th>13</th>
</tr>
</tbody>
</table>
```

- scoped. A boolean attribute to indicate whether the styles apply to the entire document or just the parent subtree.
- seamless. The purpose of this attribute is to make the included document appear to be part of the orginal document and not to appear as if if were a quotation from another source (which, nevertheless, it is!) Not to be recommended to University students writing up their thesis.
- selected. When the attribute selected is chosen for an option, then that value will be the value selected as the default. It can be changed by the user.
  Example:

Choose a day:
```
Sunday
Monday
Tuesday
Wednesday
Thursday
Friday
Saturday
```

and the markup:

```
<p>Choose a day:
<select name="weekday">
  <option value="Sunday">Sunday</option>
  <option selected="selected" value="Monday">Monday</option>
  <option value="Tuesday">Tuesday</option>
  <option value="Wednesday">Wednesday</option>
  <option value="Thursday">Thursday</option>
  <option value="Friday">Friday</option>
  <option value="Saturday">Saturday</option>
</select></p>
```

- shape. This defines the shape of the <area> which you wish to display. It can take three values only:
  - rect or rectangle
  - circ or circle
  - poly or polygon

The missing value defaults to *rectangle*. Example:

```
<img src="demonstration.jpg" usemap="#demo"
     alt="This is a rectangle with no special peculiarites">
<map name="demo">
  <area shape="rect" coords="25,25,85,85">
</map>
```

- size. For the <input> element it defines the number of characters that the user can see. For the <select> element it defines the number of options the user can see.
  Example: *size=20*
- sizes attribute. This defines the possible sizes of an image when used with the <source> element when it is part of a <picture> element. Example:

sizes="(min-width: 600px) 25vw, (min-width: 500px) 50vw, 100vw"

vw is a style sheet unit. The w stands for width and h would stand for height. v represents the viewport (the viewing area). 1 unit refects 1/100th the width of the viewport so to make an image the full width of the viewport it would be set to 100vw. This is the default.

- sortable. This enables a sorting interface for the table.
- sorted. The column sort direction. Normal without 'reversed', otherwise the opposite direction. Only for use with the element <th>.
- span. This defines the number of columns the <col> should span.
- src. This is necessary with the elements <video>, <audio>, <embed>, <iframe>, <img> and <source> to define the address of the resource, a valid URL, to be shown or embedded.
- srcdoc. A document (the source) to be rendered within an <iframe>.
- srclang. The Language of the text track.
- srcset. Used with the <source> element when it is used with the <picture> element. It consists of zero or more image sources (URLs), a source size and optionally a media query.
- start. The first line of an ordered list normally starts with the number '1'. However there may be a reason to start with a different value. This can be done by using the attribute start. To give an example let's consider an index which is 80 pages long (a list of names of the members of a family consisting of 4,000 people). This list starts for the letter 'A' with the first person, Albert Abbott and the 'A's finish at the 219th person Lillie Auton. For clarity reasons it seems a good idea to divide the list by the first letter of each surname.

A

1. *Albert Abbott - [1885]*
2. *Arthur W Abbott - [1874]*
3. *Clarice Abbott - [1911]*
4. *Elijah Abbott - [1880]*
   ...
217. *Elizabeth Betty Auton - [?]*
218. *John Auton - [1845]*
219. *Lillie Auton - [?]*

B

220. *Jack Baddiley - [1907-1936]*
221. *James Baddiley - [1881]*
222. *John Edmund Baddiley - [1886 - 1890]*
223. *John Edward Baddiley - [1860]*

The markup for this is:

```
<h3>A</h3>
<ol>
<li>Albert Abbott<em> - [1885]</em></li>
<li>Arthur W Abbott<em> - [1874]</em></li>
<li>Clarice Abbott<em> - [1911]</em></li>
<li>Elijah Abbott<em> - [1880]</em></li>
```

```
</ol>
  ...
<ol start=217>
  <li>Elizabeth Betty Auton<em> - [?]</em></li>
  <li>John Auton<em> - [1845]</em></li>
  <li>Lillie Auton<em> - [?]</em></li>
</ol>
<h3>B</h3>
<ol start=220>
  <li>Jack Baddiley<em> - [1907-1936]</em></li>
  <li>James Baddiley<em> - [1881]</em></li>
  <li>John Edmund Baddiley<em> - [1886 - 1890]</em></li>
  <li>John Edward Baddiley<em> - [1860]</em></li>
</ol>
```

- step. This attribute indicates the granularity that is expected of the value attribute for the `<input>` element.

*Example of the **step** attribute:*

and the markup:

```
<p class="markup"><label>Example of the <code>step</code>
        attribute:
        <input type="number" min="7" max="25" step="2">
        </label></p>
```

- target. A linked page is normally displayed in the current browser window unless another target is specified. Permissable values are:
    - _self
    - _parent
    - _top
    - _blank
    - any string that does not start with an underscore provided that that string exists as a browsing context name

Examples:
    - self - same window
    - parent - new window
    - top - topmost window in a frameset, otherwise same window
    - blank - new tab
    - string myiframe - in the iframe named myiframe

and the markup:

```
<ul>
  <li><a target=_self href="http://www.managers-net.org">
      self - same window</a></li>
  <li><a target=_parent href="http://www.managers-net.org">
      parent - new window</a></li>
```

```
<li><a target=_top href="http://www.managers-net.org">
    top - topmost window in a frameset,
        otherwise same window</a></li>
<li><a target=_blank href="http://www.managers-net.org">
    blank - New tab</a></li>
<li><a target=myiframe href="http://www.managers-net.org">
    string myiframe - in the iframe named myiframe</a></li>
</ul>
```

Personally I don't like links opening in a new window or in a new tab and this is not an attribute I like to use.

* type

Element	Keywords			Action
button	submit	reset	button	controls the behaviour of the button. The keyword 'button' does nothing
command	command	checkbox	radio	indicates the kind of command
menu	context	toolbar	list	indicates the kind of menu to be shown
a	No keywords			purely advisory
area				purely advisory
embed				indicates the type of file to embed
object	Specify the resource or media type			specifies the type of resource which will be shown
source				specifies the type of media resource being requested

For the `<input>` element the `type` attribute has about 23 different possible keywords:

Keyword	keyword=
hidden	An arbitrary string
text	Text with no line breaks
search	Text with no line breaks
tel	Text (telephone no) with no line breaks
url	A web address
email	An e-mail address or list of e-mail addresses
password	Text with no line breaks. The password will not be shown
datetime	A date and time (year, month, day, hour, minute, second, fraction of a second) with the time zone set to GMT (UTC)
date	A date (year, month, day) with no time zone
month	A date consisting of a year and a month with no time zone
week	A date consisting of a week-year number and a week number with no time zone
time	A time (hour, minute, seconds, fractional seconds) with no time zone
datetime-local	A date and time (year, month, day, hour, minute, second, fraction of a second) with no time zone
number	A numerical value
range	A numerical value, but the exact value is not important
color	An sRGB color with 8-bit red, green, and blue components
checkbox	A predefined list from which one or more choices may be made
radio	A predefined list from which only one value may be selected (unless the `multiple` attribute is used)
file	A file name
submit	none - 'type="submit"'
image	Another way of submitting the data
reset	none - used to cancel the data entry and start again if desired
button	none - simply a button which does nothing!

- `typemustmatch`. A boolean attribute to show whether the `type` attribute and the content-type value need to match in order for the resource to be used. Of especial use for resources called from another domain for security purposes.
- `usemap` is used to define the map to be used for the `<map>` element. This will be used with all the `<area>` elements associated with this map.

  Let's assume that you wish to select a web page by clicking on a triangle. Your shape is a triangle. and the image is in a file called triangle_in_picture.jpg.

  Let the coordinates of the triangle be at the points 10, 10; 30, 50 and 50, 10 in the picture.

  Here is the markup:

  ```
  <img src="triangle_in_picture.jpg"
    usemap="#triangle"
    alt="This should be a picture of a triangle.">
  <map name="triangle">
   <area shape=polygon
      coords="10,10,30,50,50,10"
      href="web_page.html"
      alt="triangle">
  </map>
  ```

  Note that the name for `map` and `usemap` must be the same, in this case "triangle".
- `value` is one of six attributes used by the `<meter>` element. The other attributes are `low`, `high`, `min`, `max` and `optimum`.
  - The `min` attribute specifies the lower bound of the range,
  - the `max` attribute specifies the upper bound of the range,
  - the `value` attribute specifies the "measured" value which the gauge should indicate,
  - the `low` attribute specifies what is considered a "low" value whilst
  - the `high` attribute specifies what is considered to be the "high" value.
  - The `optimum` attribute shows the position of the gauge which is considered to be the "optimum".

  Not all the attributes need to be specified.

  These examples are equivalent:

  ```
  <meter>75%</meter>
  <meter min="0" max="100" value="75"></meter>
  ```

- `width` and `height` attributes may be specified to give the dimensions of the picture or image which you wish to display. They are not intended to stretch the image, indeed, if you wish to display an image using the

`<img>` element it is better to resize the picture using a program such as 'The Gimp' and then to omit these attributes altogether.
An example of the markup is:

> *<embed src="../actionwork/bullying.avi" height=150 width=100>*

- `wrap`. When using

<textarea wrap="soft"></textarea>

the text in the box is wrapped but is not sent wrapped, it is sent as one long string. This is the default value. The only other value is "hard" which means that the text in the box is wrapped and is sent wrapped. When using this value, the `cols` attribute must also be used, for example:

Enter your text

The markup is:

> *<textarea wrap="hard" cols=60>Enter your text</textarea>*

Detailed description of the use of the element
`<Canvas>`

An artist uses a canvas, usually, on which to paint pictures. This is the first thing we need here as well:

```
<canvas></canvas>
```

and we need to describe its size (width and height for a 2 dimensional object):

```
<canvas width="800" height="450"></canvas>
```

but just in case there is a problem or the browser is unable to display the element `<Canvas>` we need to add a warning:

```
<canvas width="800" height="450">
Your browser does not support Canvas</canvas>
```

To show the size of the canvas I have added in a border:

```
<canvas width="800" height="450" style="border: 1px solid #000000">
Your browser does not support Canvas</canvas>
```

Let's put something on the canvas. To do this we need to write a script using the element `<script>`, thus:

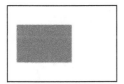

```
<canvas id="tableau1" width="120" height="80" style="border: 1px solid
#000000">
Your browser does not support Canvas</canvas>
<script>
var thisdoc = document.getElementById("tableau1");
```

```
var box = thisdoc.getContext("2d");
box.fillStyle="red";
box.fillRect(10,20,60,40);
</script>
```

or we could put a coloured circle inside:

```
<canvas id="tableau2" width="120" height="80" style="border: 1px solid
#000000">
Your browser does not support Canvas</canvas>
<script>
var c=document.getElementById("tableau2");
var box=c.getContext("2d");
    (a 2 dimensional rectangle)
var x_coord = tableau2.width / 2;
var y_coord = tableau2.height / 2;
    (the x and y coordinates for the centre of the circle)
var radius = 30;
box.beginPath();
box.arc(x_coord, y_coord, radius, 0, 2*Math.PI);
    (the 0, the fourth parameter, is the starting angle in radians - starts at 3
o'clock)
    (2*Math.PI is the ending angle of the arc, clockwise - 1*Math.PI would
produce a semicircle)
    (To make it go anticlockwise, add another parameter, 'true')
box.fillStyle = "yellow";
box.fill();
</script>
```

with a blue border around it

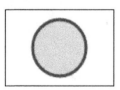

```
<canvas id="tableau3" width="120" height="80" style="border: 1px solid
#000000">
Your browser does not support Canvas</canvas>
<script>
var c=document.getElementById("tableau3");
```

```
var box=c.getContext("2d");
var x_coord = tableau3.width / 2;
var y_coord = tableau3.height / 2;
var radius = 30;
box.beginPath();
box.arc(x_coord, y_coord, radius, 0, 2*Math.PI);
box.fillStyle = "yellow";
box.fill();
   (add these lines:)
box.lineWidth = 1;
box.strokeStyle = "blue";
box.stroke();
</script>
```

Now let's add some text inside:

```
   (just add these lines after 'box.stroke();')
box.fillStyle = "red";
box.fillText("Hi there", 40, 45);
```

Finally, before we leave you to explore `<Canvas>` on your own, let's show a photograph using `<Canvas>`. I know that it can also be done simply using the element `<img>` outside `<Canvas>`.

```
   ()
<script>
window.onload = function()
   {
```

```
getPhoto();
}
function getPhoto()
    (First we need to get the picture)
{
picture = new Image();
picture.src = "/swanage.jpg"
picture.addEventListener('load', drawPicture);
    (The program won't continue until the picture is fully loaded)
}
function drawPicture()
    (This puts the picture on the canvas)
{
var c = document.getElementById("tableau5");
var box=c.getContext("2d");
box.drawImage(picture, 0, 0);
    (The last two paramters are the x & y coordinates for the starting
position of the picture)
}
</script>
```

Obsolete elements

HTML is backwards compatible, that means that these obsolete elements will still work, however if you try to validate your web page (use *http://html5.validator.nu/*), these will show up as errors.

The following elements are purely presentational and are better handled by CSS:

- basefont
- big
- blink
- center
- font
- marquee - CSS transistions and animations (gif files) are more appropriate
- plaintext - use the "*text/plain*" MIME type instead
- spacer
- strike. Use `<del>` instead for editing, otherwise `<s>`
- tt

The following elements have been removed from HTML because they affect usability and accessibility by the user negatively.

Use `<iframe>` and CSS instead or if the intention is to keep a menu or a heading on every page, create new pages instead of `<frame>`s and use server-side includes (SSI) to include these menus or headings on each page.

- frame
- frameset
- noframes

The following elements are rarely used, create confusion and are better handled by other elements:

- acronym - use `<abbr>` instead
- appplet - use `<embed>` or `<object>` instead
- command - use `<menuitem>` instead
- isindex - use an explicit `<form>` and text field combination instead
- dir - use `<ul>` instead
- xmp - use `<pre>` and `<code>` instead
- noembed - use `<object>` instead of `<embed>` when fallback is necessary

The following attribute is unnecessary. Omit it altogether:

- target on `<link>` elements

Some dont's

Authors must not use elements, attributes and attribute values for purposes other than their appropriate intended semantic purpose, for example, tables should only be used for tabular data, not as place holders for presentation purposes. CSS is the appropriate tool for presentation.

Do not use frames, but you can use the `<iframe>` element (see page 82)

The old `<center>` element is obsolete. Use CSS instead

Index